Pathfinders

Pathfinders

THE JOURNEYS OF 16 EXTRAORDINARY BLACK SOULS

Tonya Bolden

ABRAMS BOOKS FOR YOUNG READERS
NEW YORK

- - - - - - - - - - - - - - - - → For Rodney J. Reynolds and Audrey Peterson, publisher and editor of *American Legacy* magazine, this book's inspiration

Library of Congress Cataloging-in-Publication Data

Names: Bolden, Tonya, author.
Title: Pathfinders : The amazing journey of 16 extraordinary black souls / Tonya Bolden.
Description: New York : Abrams Books for Young Readers, 2017. | Includes bibliographical references and index. | Audience: Age 10 to 14.
Identifiers: LCCN 2015043356 | ISBN 9781419714559
Subjects: LCSH: African Americans—Biography—Juvenile literature. | Successful people—United States—Biography—Juvenile literature.
Classification: LCC E185.96 .B569 2016 | DDC 920.0092/96073—dc23
LC record available at http://lccn.loc.gov/2015043356

Text copyright © 2017 Tonya Bolden
Book design by Think Studio: thinkstudionyc.com

OPPOSITE TITLE PAGE: *Aspiration* (1936), oil on canvas, by Aaron Douglas. This painting features a man standing beside a globe holding a carpenter's angle and a compass, another man with a chemistry beaker, and a woman with a book. They stand upon a plinth, raised above shackled arms, looking forward to a great city on a hill. Our three sojourners are on a quest for success.

For illustration credits, see page 117.

Printed and bound in China
10 9 8 7 6 5 4 3 2

Abrams Books for Young Readers are available at special discounts when purchased in quantity for premiums and promotions as well as fundraising or educational use. Special editions can also be created to specification. For details, contact specialsales@abramsbooks.com or the address below.

ABRAMS The Art of Books
115 West 18th Street, New York, NY 10011
abramsbooks.com

Grit. Guts. Goals.

Over the centuries countless blacks in America have done amazing things against the odds. Had big, bold dreams. Pursued passions. Caught up with their callings. Charted courses to success. Pathfinders.

In this book you'll find sketches of sixteen such people. Here you will meet a man who made magic along with one who believed that he could fly and a woman of great mystery. Here you will meet people who went on adventures, took chances, maximizing their talents and abilities. More than a few had a lot to overcome. More than a few knew hardships and tragedies when young.

To round out their stories, there are sidebars with tidbits of history—not everything that happened during a subject's lifetime, just a sampling of events that made up the context of his or her life. With these sketches you will also find brief mentions of people (and in one case places) who have something in common with the subject, to underscore that this architect or that mathematician was not alone in a profession or pursuit. Not an isolated success.

Most of these Pathfinders have been dear to my heart for years. A few I learned about relatively recently from *American Legacy* magazine. Whether old acquaintances or new, all inspire me. All remind me that so much is possible. May their journeys motivate you to dream, reach, soar—become a Pathfinder yourself! Above all, as W.E.B. Du Bois, trailblazing scholar-activist best known for his book *The Souls of Black Folk*, urged, "As you live, believe in Life!"

A NARRATIVE

OF THE

LIFE & ADVENTURES

OF

VENTURE,

A NATIVE OF AFRICA;

BUT RESIDENT ABOVE SIXTY YEARS IN THE
UNITED STATES OF AMERICA.

RELATED BY HIMSELF.

NEW LONDON—PRINTED IN 1798.

RE-PRINTED, A. D. 1835,

AND PUBLISHED BY A

DESCENDANT OF VENTURE.

Venture **Smith**

c. 1727–1805

Born Broteer Furro, this eldest son of a prince was proud of his heritage, proud to be an African. Had he not been, he might never have survived years of ordeals and, in the end, triumphed.

Broteer was ten or so when members of an enemy tribe raided his West African village. When the attack was over, his father was dead and he, bludgeoned and roped, a captive. Next came a four-hundred-mile forced march to the coast, imprisonment in a slave castle's dungeon, then confinement on the *Charming Susanna*, a slave ship.

OPPOSITE The title page of Venture Smith's memoir. This edition was published by a relative years after Venture's death.

With Broteer and ninety other Africans, the *Charming Susanna* set sail in late spring 1739. Some seventy days and one smallpox outbreak later, it docked at Bridgetown, Barbados. There, most of the seventy-four kidnapped Africans who had survived the gruesome journey were sold to planters.

Broteer was not among them. A ship's officer, Robinson Mumford, had already bought him for four gallons of rum and a piece of calico. Mumford decided to start the boy's American life in Newport, Rhode Island, where a sister of his would have the task of teaching the child English and how to be a slave.

So there Broteer was in September 1739, in a strange world, around strange people, and coming to terms with a strange, new name: Venture. Mumford renamed him that because he had purchased the boy "with his own private venture" (that is, capital, such as goods or cash).

The attack on Venture's village; the murder of his father; Venture's abduction; his separation from his mother, his siblings, his friends, his people; the fetid hold of the *Charming Susanna*; the abuse from different owners in Newport, then on Fishers Island in Long Island Sound, then in Stonington, Connecticut, then in Hartford, then in Stonington again—

Nothing broke Venture's spirit. Nothing destroyed his will to be free again, his refusal to be a slave.

In 1761, when he was in his early thirties, Venture, standing over six feet tall and weighing about three hundred pounds, convinced his fifth owner, the Stonington shipbuilder and merchant Oliver Smith Jr., to let him buy his freedom. With the bargain struck, as a poet put it, Venture "spun money out of sweat."

Sweat from nighttime seine fishing and lobster trapping, then selling his catch.

Sweat from daytime planting and harvesting of produce to peddle.

Sweat from chopping and stacking four hundred cords of firewood—at least a thousand *tons*—during a six-month stint on Long Island.

Sweat from these sideline jobs *atop* labors for his owner.

Come spring 1765, after four years of paying for himself in installments, Venture had his liberty—for seventy-one pounds and two shillings, the cost of hundreds of

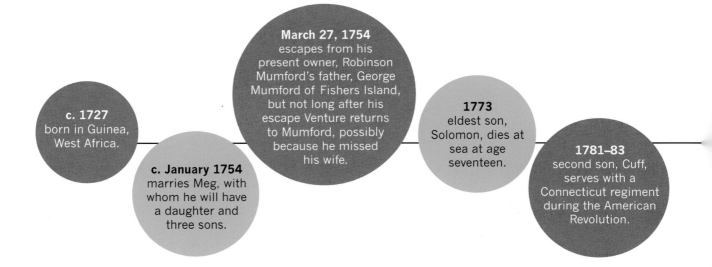

c. 1727
born in Guinea, West Africa.

c. January 1754
marries Meg, with whom he will have a daughter and three sons.

March 27, 1754
escapes from his present owner, Robinson Mumford's father, George Mumford of Fishers Island, but not long after his escape Venture returns to Mumford, possibly because he missed his wife.

1773
eldest son, Solomon, dies at sea at age seventeen.

1781–83
second son, Cuff, serves with a Connecticut regiment during the American Revolution.

ABOVE *South View of Mount Tom and the Mouth of Salmon River*, engraving by John Warner Barber, from his book *Connecticut Historical Collections* (1836). In *Making Freedom*, their book about Venture Smith, Chandler B. Saint and George A. Krimsky tell us that Venture Smith's homestead was "on the ridge to the left of the sailboat in the center background."

LEFT *A View of Cabo Corso Castle*, engraving by Johannes Kip, from Awnsham and John Churchill's *A Collection of Voyages and Travels . . .* volume 5 (1744). "*Cabo corso*" is Portuguese for "cape coast." This slave castle (or large slave-trading fort) was one of about forty that Europeans built on West Africa's Gold Coast (present-day Ghana) from the 1480s through the 1780s. Before Venture was taken across the Atlantic Ocean, he was held in a slave castle in the Gold Coast town of Anomabu.

c. 1782
daughter, Hannah, dies.

September 19, 1805
dies in Haddam Neck, Connecticut.

After the French and Indian War (1754–1763) between French and British forces (with both sides aided by American colonists and Indians), Britain's holdings in North America more than doubled. France ceded Canada and also the land between the Appalachians and the Mississippi River, which eventually became a number of U.S. states. Spain, France's ally, ceded Florida. The French and Indian War became part of the Seven Years' War (1756–1763) between France and Britain and their European allies. Although Britain emerged the victor, with enormous territorial gains in various parts of the world, the war left this great power in deep debt. To reduce it, Britain imposed more and more taxes on the Thirteen Colonies, lighting the fuse for the American Revolution (1775–1783).

One of several events leading up to the American Revolution occurred on the night of March 5, 1770: the Boston Massacre. When British soldiers fired into a crowd of disgruntled colonists, black seafarer Crispus Attucks was the first one killed. He is regarded as the first casualty of the Revolution.

When a London firm released her *Poems on Various Subjects, Religious and Moral* on September 1, 1773, West African–born Phillis Wheatley, about age twenty, became the first black person to have a book of poetry published in English.

The American Revolution began on April 19, 1775, with the Battles of Lexington and Concord, about fifteen and twenty miles northwest of Boston.

On July 8, 1777, Vermont became the first former British North American possession to abolish slavery. This was nearly 140 years after Massachusetts became the first one to legalize it, in 1641.

acres of land. Business concluded, "I left Col. Smith once for all." Taking the man's last name with him, Venture geared up for another goal: to free his wife and children, all held by his third owner, another man in Stonington.

With his brawn (chopping wood, farming, fishing, whaling) and with his brains (buying and selling land at a profit, trading), Venture Smith had his entire family out of slavery by spring 1775. He also had a place for them to live: ten acres overlooking Salmon River Cove in Haddam Neck, Connecticut. He built a home, a farm, and a boatyard in that village. He eventually owned more than one hundred acres.

Venture Smith labored less and less as the years rolled by. With his body bent by time and toil and his eyesight failing, he relied on grandchildren to help him get around when old. Though his Herculean strength was spent, he still had his wits and wanted to tell his story. With a local white schoolteacher, Elisha Niles, serving as his scribe, he got it done. The result was a slim memoir published in 1798 called *A Narrative of the Life and Adventures of Venture, a Native of Africa*. Millions of Africans journeyed to the early Americas by force or by choice; only about a dozen wrote memoirs that survive.

"I was born at Dukandarra, in Guinea," begins Venture Smith's. "My father's name was Saungm Furro, Prince of the Tribe of Dukandarra. . . . I descended from a very large, tall and stout race of beings, much larger than the generality of people in other parts of the globe."

Guinea was not a country then but a region. It comprised today's Benin, the Gambia, Ghana, Senegal, and several other nations. While scholars have deduced that this eldest son of a prince was born in or near present-day Ghana, they have yet to unearth anything about the Dukandarra people. Some have concluded that the extraordinary Broteer Furro / Venture Smith descended from a now-lost tribe.

Also in Colonial America

Connecticut-born **Abijah Prince** (c. 1706–94) saved his money, too. After he was freed from slavery in Northfield, Massachusetts, Prince moved to nearby Deerfield. There, in May 1746, he married **Lucy Terry** (1724–1821), a talented poet and storyteller. Her poem "Bar's Fight," about an Indian attack on Deerfield in August 1746, is the earliest known poem by an African living in what became the United States. Lucy Terry was about five when she was kidnapped from West Africa, then sold into slavery in Rhode Island. She regained her liberty when she was in her twenties, about a year after she married Abijah Prince, who quite possibly bought her freedom. The couple eventually owned a lot of land—at one point, three hundred acres in Guilford, Vermont.

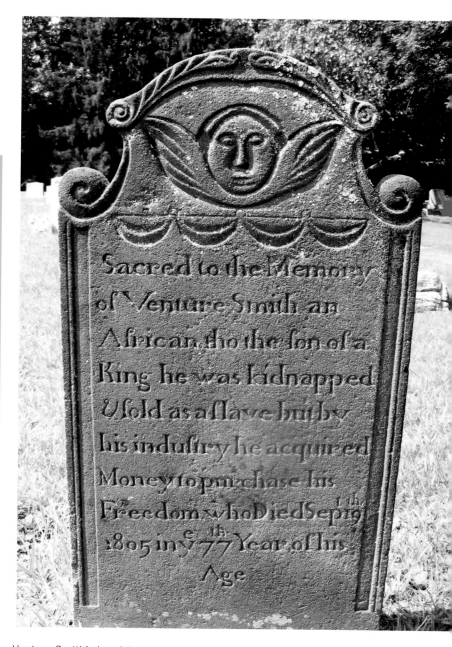

Venture Smith's headstone, carved by John Isham and photographed by David C. Nelson. The cherub's nose is broader and its mouth fuller than those on other headstones the carver made. Did Isham create this more African image out of respect for Venture Smith or on his command? Also unknown is why Smith is here identified as the son of a king instead of the son of a prince. Smith was buried in the cemetery of East Haddam's First Congregational Church, a white church.

ENTREPRENEUR

James **Forten**

1766–1842

After more than two hundred days in Hell, he was homeward-bound at last.

Two years earlier, in the summer of 1781, James Forten had become an American revolutionary by signing on as a powder boy with a privateer, the *Royal Louis*. Like other private ships aiding the Continental Navy, this twenty-two-gun sloop's mission was to hunt down and plunder British merchant ships. Like his mates, freeborn Forten, nearly fifteen, was all gung ho—and not just because he was a Patriot. He expected to get a share of the prize money from the plunder, money his family desperately needed.

OPPOSITE This c. 1840 daguerreotype by an unidentified photographer is believed to be of James Forten, who was born James Fortune. No one knows for certain why he changed his surname.

September 2, 1766
born in Philadelphia, Pennsylvania, to a free black man and a woman who may have been enslaved before she bore her first child.

November 10, 1803
marries Martha Beatte, who will die in six months.

December 10, 1805
marries Charlotte Vandine, a teacher, with whom he will have four boys and five girls.

March 24, 1814
second child and second daughter, Charlotte, dies at age five.

March 4, 1842
dies in Philadelphia, Pennsylvania.

Interior of the Old Jersey Prison Ship, in the Revolutionary War, engraving by Edward Bookhout of an illustration by Felix Octavius Carr Darley, from Henry Howe's *Life and Death on the Ocean: A Collection of Extraordinary Adventures* (1855). During that war, about 11,000 Patriots died aboard British prison ships, whereas about 4,400 died in combat.

The *Royal Louis* was successful in its first cruise, but in its second it became the prey of a thirty-two-gun British warship, the *Amphion*. After the sloop's capture off the coast of Virginia in October 1781, its crew of 200 men and boys, branded pirates, became prisoners. Young James was among the 130 or so transferred to the *Amphion*—and headed for a truly dreadful place: the *Jersey*, an unseaworthy British vessel, which was moored in New York's Wallabout Bay.

Aboard the *Amphion*, Forten became chums with the captain's twelve-year-old son, Henry Bazely. Captain Bazely had coaxed the two into that friendship to keep his son occupied and out of trouble. The captain came to admire Forten so much that he offered to take him to England, where the Bazely family would be his benefactor in getting an education and advancing in life. Aware that the British often sold black prisoners into slavery in the West Indies, Forten, nevertheless, declined the captain's offer. "I have been taken prisoner for the liberties of my country, and never will prove a traitor to her interest," he said. The young Patriot, who had been present for the first public reading of the Declaration of Independence back on July 8, 1776, was soon prisoner number 4102 aboard the *Jersey*.

The *Jersey* was an overcrowded, pestilential place. The meager rations of moldy bread. The lice. The ticks. The awful stench. The sight of festering sores. The corpses hurled overboard. The hulk was known as "Hell." And young Forten endured it for seven long months, until the spring of 1782, when he was released in a prisoner exchange.

Home!

He was skin and bones.

Home!

He was nearly bald from scurvy.

Home!

On that spring day in Wallabout Bay, James Forten was determined to make it home to Philadelphia, about eighty miles away, where his mother and older sister, also free, were surely fretting and frantic.

Home!

For years young Forten had been a breadwinner. He was about nine years old when he left school to work (sweeping up and doing other odd jobs in a shop).

Home!

Adding to his misery, he was barefoot for most of his trek. He didn't luck upon a pair of shoes until he reached Trenton, New Jersey.

Home!

About thirty miles later he made it.

Home!

His mother, Margaret, and sister, Abigail, nursed him back to health in the small wooden house they rented near the corner of Third and Walnut Streets, not far from the Delaware River.

Twenty-four years after that long walk from New York to Philadelphia, James Forten was not only a healthy man but a prosperous one, too—and with a big family. Home now was a large three-story brick house that Forten owned on Lombard Street, blocks away from his thriving business. He had become a success by following in his father's footsteps.

Forten's father, Thomas, had been a sailmaker for Robert Bridges, the son of Irish immigrants. When James was a kid, his father took him to work with him at Bridges's sail loft on Willings' Wharf. There, father began teaching son the ABCs of sail making,

IN HIS TIME

Philadelphia's Carpenters' Hall was home to the First Continental Congress (September 5–October 26, 1774). During these meetings John Adams, George Washington, and delegates from other colonies hashed out how to respond to British tyranny. One action they took was to draft a letter to King George III threatening to boycott British goods if he did not abolish the Intolerable Acts, retaliatory measures (like putting Massachusetts under military rule) in response to the Boston Tea Party (December 16, 1773).

The Second Continental Congress (May 10, 1775–March 1, 1781) had its first session in Philadelphia's State House (now Independence Hall) less than a month after the American Revolution began with the Battles of Lexington and Concord. In the first session (May 10, 1775–December 12, 1776), the governing body of the Thirteen Colonies created the Continental Army, drafted George Washington to head it, and issued the Declaration of Independence.

On March 1, 1780, the Pennsylvania legislature passed an act for the gradual abolition of slavery in the colony. People born into slavery after that date became indentured servants to be freed at age twenty-eight. People born before that date would remain enslaved until they died unless their owners chose to free them. The same applied to boys and girls born after March 1, 1780, who were owned by members of Congress, foreign diplomats, and consuls.

The United States Constitution was signed on September 17, 1787, in Philadelphia, the nation's capital from early December 1790 until mid-May 1800.

Pennsylvania's state constitution of 1838 restricted the right to vote to free white men.

Another Enterprising Mind

Born free in Warwick, Rhode Island, **Elleanor Eldridge** (1785–1862) entered the work world at the age of ten, then proceeded to amass skills and money. She was a housekeeper, quilter, spinner, weaver, cheese maker, soap maker, house painter, wallpaper hanger—and more. By 1831, Eldridge owned property in Providence, Rhode Island, valued at about $4,000 (equivalent to about $87,000 today). When ruthless individuals tried to swindle her out of some of her holdings, she prevailed in court. Eldridge raised money for her legal expenses by putting out a book in 1838: *Memoirs of Elleanor Eldridge*, written by a white writer and ally, Frances H. Whipple. Eldridge's memoir had seven more printings by 1848. By then its sequel, *Elleanor's Second Book* (1839), had seen five printings.

Arch Street Ferry, Philadelphia, engraving by W. Birch & Son, from *The City of Philadelphia . . . as It Appeared in the Year 1800*, also known as *Birch's Views of Philadelphia* (1800). Young Forten and his family lived a few blocks away from this busy, bustling waterfront.

such as the best way to cut canvas, the correct way to stitch, and the safest way to handle tools such as awls, prickers, and fids. Those lessons didn't last long, because his father died when he was seven—hence the family's poverty—but they definitely came in handy later on.

About three years after he walked away from Wallabout Bay, and following another stint at sea with a merchant ship and a brief stay in England, nineteen-year-old Forten embarked on a proper apprenticeship at Bridges's shop. He was the firm's only black worker at the time.

On his way to success, Forten became as skilled at assessing the quality of a piece of canvas as he was at turning that cloth into main sails, topsails, staysails, moonsails, crossjacks, flying jibs, and more. And Forten's rise was rapid: apprentice, supervisor, junior partner, then owner in 1798, when Bridges retired. His mentor even helped him secure the loan that made the purchase possible. Forten was thirty-two when Robert Bridges and Co. became James Forten and Co.

Forten ran a tight ship, but by all accounts he was a

good boss. A visitor to his lofts in 1835 looked in on one of them and found that "all was order and harmony." At a time when many whites refused to work for blacks, about half of the twenty or thirty employees the visitor observed were white.

Through his successful sail-making business, real estate investments, and other ventures, the diligent, disciplined James Forten became one of Philadelphia's wealthiest residents. In the early 1830s he was worth an estimated $100,000, the equivalent of about $2 million today.

Generous with his riches, Forten supported his mother until she died in 1806 and his sister and her four children after her husband died in 1805. He also gave substantial sums to charities such as the Free African Society and to abolitionist organizations such as the interracial American Anti-Slavery Society, established in Philadelphia's Adelphi Hall in 1833.

Much admired in his day as an entrepreneur, philanthropist, and pillar of Philadelphia's black community, James Forten was greatly mourned when he died. One of the city's newspapers ran his obituary under the title "Death of an Excellent Man."

A Sail-Loft down in Maine, hand-colored engraving of a drawing by J. MacDonald, from the October 17, 1885, issue of *Harper's Weekly*. Forten's sail lofts probably didn't look all that different from the one seen here, except that his workers were not all white, as the men depicted here appear to be.

Richard **Potter**

1783–1835

Crawl through a solid log?

Fry pancakes in a top hat?

Dance on eggs without causing a single crack?

This was some of the abracadabra performed by Richard Potter, the first magician born in the United States to have success in the land of his birth. But it wasn't here that he found his calling.

Born some thirty miles west of Boston, Massachusetts, Richard Potter was about fifteen when he shoved off for England as a cabin boy for a Captain Skinner. He wasn't in London for long before he skipped out on the captain and, according to tradition, joined a circus, latching onto John Rannie, a famous magician and ventriloquist.

OPPOSITE
Frontispiece from the 1830 edition of Henry Dean's *The Whole Art of Legerdemain, or Hocus Pocus Laid Open and Explained.* Like other magicians of his time, Richard Potter may have owned a copy of this book.

Young Potter traveled around Europe with Rannie, they say. And when, in 1801, Rannie embarked on what would be a ten-year tour of the United States, Potter, then seventeen, was most likely with him. Not long after the master magician retired to his native Scotland, presto chango, there was Richard Potter staying in the States—stepping out on his own.

"He will present a dollar . . . and, by using no other means than touching it with his finger, make it become *forty plates*," announced a July 2, 1811, newspaper ad. Turning a silver dollar into forty plates was just one act of legerdemain (sleight of hand) that Potter was to perform that night at a hall in Newburgh, New York.

He entertained audiences in halls and taverns in Boston, Salem, and Newburyport, Massachusetts; in Providence, Rhode Island; in New Haven, Connecticut. His show in Newburgh was not his one and only in upstate New York—Potter also performed in Albany and in Hudson. When down in New York City, he sometimes played at Tammany Hall. Some sources say Potter wowed audiences with his hocus-pocus as far north as Canada and as far south as New Orleans, Louisiana. Early on, a ticket to a show cost twenty-five cents, which was the price of a pound of coffee, so not exactly cheap in those days.

Potter's audiences often included children. The great Oliver Wendell Holmes Sr., poet, physician, and professor, wrote of "endless supplies of treasures from empty hats" and of other magic tricks that "sent many a child home thinking that Mr. Potter must have ghostly assistants."

Holmes's cousin Henry Kemble Oliver, a politician, remembered the magician even better. That's because early in his career, when Potter wasn't on the road, he did domestic work for the Olivers in their Boston home. Henry Oliver recalled Potter having several big books on magic and inviting "us children to the kitchen to see his tricks and hearken to his ventriloquism."

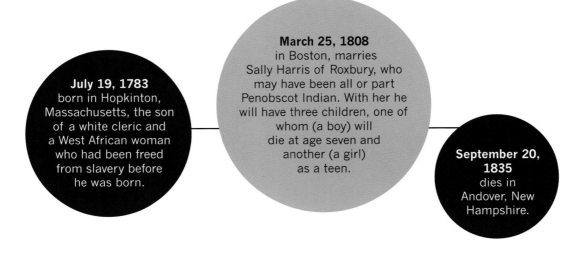

July 19, 1783 born in Hopkinton, Massachusetts, the son of a white cleric and a West African woman who had been freed from slavery before he was born.

March 25, 1808 in Boston, marries Sally Harris of Roxbury, who may have been all or part Penobscot Indian. With her he will have three children, one of whom (a boy) will die at age seven and another (a girl) as a teen.

September 20, 1835 dies in Andover, New Hampshire.

22 Or, Hocus Pocus *in Perfection.*

How to make three little children dance in a glass upon a table.

The United States just about doubled in size with the Louisiana Purchase (1803): 530 million acres from France for $15 million. Out of this vast territory the U.S. government will eventually create all or part of the following states: Arkansas, Colorado, Iowa, Kansas, Louisiana, Minnesota, Missouri, Montana, Nebraska, New Mexico, North Dakota, Oklahoma, South Dakota, Texas, and Wyoming.

The importation of slaves into the United States became illegal on January 1, 1808.

In its second war of independence, the United States declared war on Britain in June 1812. The War of 1812 ended with the signing of the Treaty of Ghent on December 24, 1814.

Ventriloquists did not use dummies back then. It was piles of hay, trees, boxes, horses, pigs, and dogs that Potter magically made talk.

In time, Potter no longer had to work for the Olivers or anybody else between tours to make ends meet. Potter did well, very well. About three years after he stepped out on his own, he bought 175 acres of farmland in Andover, New Hampshire. And he continued to prosper! A ticket to his show was up from twenty-five cents to a dollar by 1817.

When not on the road performing, Potter loved being on his farm with his family. He was crazy about the shrubs and flowers in his garden, about the crops he raised for his household and for market, about his pigs and other livestock.

They say that Potter spared no expense on his two-story main house, which he had designed himself. Downstairs were two large rooms;

LEFT Detail from a page from the 1795 edition of Henry Dean's magic book. The first edition of this classic was published in 1722, some sixty years before Richard Potter was born.

upstairs, one huge room. According to a Reverend Silas Ketchum, in this house, "finished and furnished with elegant display," Potter "kept open house, and dispensed a liberal hospitality." In another house, wrote Ketchum, "entirely separate from the [main house], was done all the cooking and housework, [and were] located all the servants' offices, . . . [and] all the sleeping-rooms."

When Richard Potter and his wife, Sally, entertained in the main house, they dazzled, decked out in fabulous, flashy outfits made of "rare and costly materials of foreign make" and in "rich and brilliant colors." So recalled Reverend Ketchum.

Some people claimed that Richard Potter was light skinned. Others said he was dark skinned. In one of the first histories of blacks in the United States, black Bostonian William Cooper Nell, about nineteen when Potter died, described the showman as "half-way between fair and black." Photography as we know it did not exist until several years after Potter died. If he ever had his portrait painted, it, like his magic kit, vanished into thin air.

HOMESTEAD of RICHARD POTTER. THE CELEBRATED VENTRILOQUIST. POTTER PLACE, N.H.

When he died, Potter was more famous for his ventriloquism than for his magic tricks. The area of Andover, New Hampshire, where he lived was named Potter Place during his lifetime. Photographer unknown.

More Black Magic

Henry "Box" Brown (c. 1816–?) is best known for his great escape from slavery in 1849 inside a small wooden crate that was shipped from Richmond, Virginia, to Philadelphia, Pennsylvania. Brown later made a name for himself as a mesmerist (hypnotist) while living in England (1850–75). When he returned to the States, he added magic to his act.

J. Hartford Armstrong (1876?–1939), a native of Spartanburg, South Carolina, was called the "King of Colored Conjurers." After he died, his daughter, Ellen, and wife, Lille Belle, carried on in the family business.

OPPOSITE A flyer for a performance by Potter on September 16, 1813 (or perhaps the year was 1818). Potter's wife, Sally, was his assistant for many years. She also sang and danced between her husband's magic tricks and acts of ventriloquism. The couple sometimes performed together in skits.

VENTRILOQUISM.

Mr. & Mrs.  POTTER,

Beg leave most respectfully to inform the Ladies and Gentlemen of *Northampton* that they will give

An Evening's Brush to sweep away Care; Or,

A MEDLEY TO PLEASE,

At Mr. *the first Ball Room near the Ready Office* Ball Room, on

Wednes day Evening, *Sept 16th 1815*

In the course of the evening will be offered upwards of

100 Curious, but Mysterious Experiments.

PART FIRST.

Mr. Potter will commence the Perform-
ance with the *Atamaton Dance*, to be followed by a number of Philo-
sophical Experiments, a few of which are here detailed.

Mr. P. will fire from a gun, any lady's or gentleman's ring, and
cause a Dove immediately to appear, in whose bill the ring will be
found. He will allow any lady or gentleman to cut their gown or
handkerchief and will unite it in such a manner that the most dis-
criminating eye cannot discover the least blemish. He will break
a number of gentlemen's Watches with a large hammer and restore
them to their regular form again. He will allow any gentleman to

draw a Card, and make the same apparently to have the appear-
ance of life, and move across the room. These are but few of the
Experiments that will be offered in the course of the evening.

Mr. P. flatters himself that his Perform-
ances have been so well known, in various parts of the Country, as
not to require the aid of a pompous advertisement; but will only
inform the ladies and gentlemen, that may wish to honor him with
their company, that this Bill can give but a faint idea of the Performance.

A SONG, by Mr. Potter.

PART SECOND.

VENTRILOQUISM.

Mr. P. will display his wonderful but laborious powers of Ventriloquism. He throws his voice into many dif-
ferent parts of the Room, and into Gentlemen's Hats, Trunks, &c. &c. Imitates all kinds of Birds and Beasts, so that few or none will be able to distinguish his Imitations from the
reality. This part of the performance has never failed of exciting the surprize of the learned and well informed, as the conveyance of Sounds is allowed to be one of the greatest curiosities in nature. *AFTER WHICH WILL BE SUNG*

THE FAVORITE SONG of by Mr. *Potter.*

PART THIRD.

WILL BE PERFORMED THE FOURTH SCENE OF THE REVIEW, OR THE

Wag of Windsor,

(WRITTEN BY COLEMAN, Jun.)

Pheabey, or the disguised Captain, with a Song, - - - - -	Mrs. *Potter.*
Caleb Quotem, with a Day's Work and Song, - - - -	Mr. *Potter.*

TO WHICH WILL BE ADDED THE PANTOMIMICAL PIECE, CALLED THE

Agreeable Surprise, or the Wonderful Little Giant,

GIANT, - - - - - - - - - - - - Mrs. *Potter.*

Mr. POTTER will add to the diversion of the Entertainment in his representation of the Comic Scenes of the CLOWN, and close with a favorite
Song in the Character of TIMOTHY NORPOST.

Tickets *12½* Cents, to be had at the place of performance. *and at Mr Lyman's Inn* Performance to commence at early candle-light. The public may rest assured that the Room will be in ample order for the reception of Visitors, handsomely illuminated, with good music during the Interludes. Ladies or Gentlemen
desirous of having seats reserved for them, are requested to send timely notice.

TRUE & ROWE, Printers, 78, Stale-street, Boston

James McCune Smith

1813–1865

"In behalf of myself and fellow schoolmates, may I be permitted to express our sincere and respectful gratitude to you for . . . visiting this institution."

That's how James, age eleven, began his welcome address to a very famous man touring the twenty-four U.S. states. The distinguished visitor was General Lafayette, a French aristocrat who had fought with the Continental Army during the American Revolution.

"I thank you, my dear child," said the general when James finished his speech.

OPPOSITE *Dr. James McCune Smith* (date unknown), engraving by his friend and former classmate Patrick Reason.

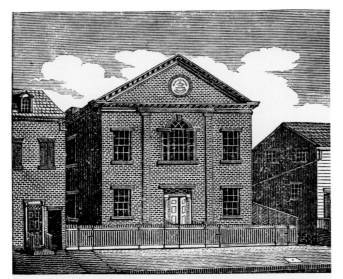

NEW-YORK AFRICAN FREE-SCHOOL, No. 2.
Engraved from a drawing taken by P. Reason, a pupil, aged 13 years.

New-York African Free-School, No. 2, frontispiece to *The History of the New-York African Free-Schools, from Their Establishment in 1787, to the Present Time* (1830), by Charles C. Andrews, one of the school's principals. The African Free-School system was created by the New York Manumission Society, an organization formed by Alexander Hamilton, the founder and first secretary of the U.S. Treasury, and other prominent white men. The African Free-School system was serving more than 1,400 girls and boys in seven buildings when it was absorbed into New York City's public school system in the early 1830s. The "P. Reason" in the engraving's caption was Smith's classmate Patrick Reason, who grew up to be an accomplished artist.

This event occurred about forty years after the Revolution, on September 10, 1824, at New York City's African Free-School No. 2, which, like other African Free-Schools, was open to both free and enslaved black children. Welcoming General Lafayette to his school was one of several honors bestowed upon James, at the time enslaved. Another was a Class of Merit medal awarded to the brightest and best-behaved pupils.

Spelling, grammar, penmanship. Astronomy, geography, geology, navigation. Of all the subjects James studied, his favorite was probably natural philosophy (science), for his great ambition was to be a physician.

When in 1828, at age fifteen, he graduated with honors from African Free-School No. 2, James, by then possessing his liberty, was still intent on being a doctor. Because fluency in Latin and ancient Greek was required for college admission, he took private lessons in those languages with a black minister, Peter Williams Jr., pastor of Saint Philip's Episcopal Church. The tutorials took place evenings. By day, Monday through Saturday, Smith worked in a blacksmith's shop. He could be seen, remembered a friend, "at a forge with the bellows in one hand and a Latin grammar [book] in the other."

After sufficient study with Reverend Williams, James applied to Geneva College in Geneva, New York (now Hobart and William Smith Colleges). That college denied him admission because of his race. So did New York City's Columbia College. Undaunted, and at Reverend Williams's urging, Smith applied to a school across the Atlantic Ocean: the University of Glasgow in Glasgow, Scotland. Accepted!

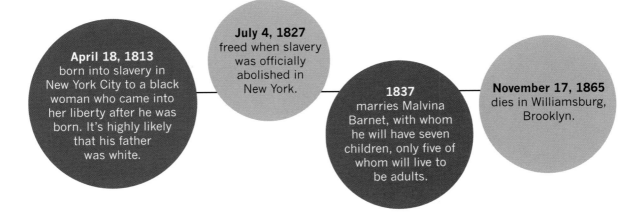

April 18, 1813
born into slavery in New York City to a black woman who came into her liberty after he was born. It's highly likely that his father was white.

July 4, 1827
freed when slavery was officially abolished in New York.

1837
marries Malvina Barnet, with whom he will have seven children, only five of whom will live to be adults.

November 17, 1865
dies in Williamsburg, Brooklyn.

The Inner Quadrangle of the Old College, University of Glasgow (1852), watercolor on paper by Samuel Bough. James McCune Smith was able to pursue his education in part because he had financial aid from the Glasgow Emancipation Society, of which he was a member. While Smith was in Scotland, slavery was abolished throughout the British Empire (1833).

IN HIS TIME

The first black-owned newspaper in the United States, *Freedom's Journal*, was established in mid-March 1827 in New York City. One of its founders was Smith's mentor, Reverend Williams. Its editors were Samuel Eli Cornish, a Presbyterian minister, and John Brown Russworm, a Jamaican educator and the third black person to graduate from an American college (Bowdoin College, Brunswick, Maine, in 1826).

In its *Dred Scott* decision on March 6, 1857, the U.S. Supreme Court ruled that blacks never were and never could be U.S. citizens and that Congress had no right to regulate slavery in the U.S. territories.

Two years into the Civil War (1861–65), a white protest of the draft for military service escalated into several days of rioting. During the New York City Draft Riots of July 1863, scores of black people were attacked, along with their homes, businesses, and institutions. The orphanage where Dr. Smith worked was one casualty. Rioters also targeted white abolitionists and government officials.

Smith got into the fourth-oldest university in the English-speaking world—a university that was more than three hundred years older than America, a university far more prestigious than Geneva and Columbia colleges. Why Reverend Williams recommended the University of Glasgow isn't clear, but we know that the cleric's help did not end there. Williams helped raise some of the money his protégé needed to attend Glasgow's glorious university.

So it was that on August 16, 1832, nineteen-year-old James McCune Smith was aboard the *Caledonia*. A few days later he wrote in his journal of a "fine breeze" that sent the ship "joyfully on her way, and curled the tops of the dark blue waves with beautiful foam-crests."

Three weeks later the *Caledonia* docked at Liverpool, England, where Smith stayed for a couple of days. He did some sightseeing. He visited acquaintances. One evening found him at a party engaged in spirited dancing— "whirling down the mazy dance." Finally, on Sunday, September 16, the young man boarded a ship bound for Glasgow.

During the next five years—five years of anatomy, botany, chemistry, logic, mathematics, natural history, natural philosophy, statistics, surgery, and more—James McCune Smith earned a bachelor's degree, a master's degree, and then, in 1837, his medical degree, graduating at the top of his class or near it with each degree. After those triumphs, he worked at the Glasgow Royal Infirmary and then at a hospital in Paris, France.

When James McCune Smith, the first black university-

His Mates

James McCune Smith was not the only graduate of African Free-School No. 2 to make giant strides. Among the others were:

Charles Reason (1818–93) was a math whiz. At the age of fourteen he was teaching some of his schoolmates. As an adult, he taught at New York Central College in McGrawville—the first black person to teach at a majority-white college in the United States. Reason later served as principal of a Quaker school in Philadelphia, Pennsylvania: the Institute for Colored Youth (now Cheyney University). Charles Reason's brothers, Elmer and Patrick, also attended African Free-School No. 2. The Reason boys were the children of a woman born in Guadeloupe and a man born in present-day Haiti. The couple had emigrated from Haiti to America in 1793, during the Haitian Revolution (1789–1804).

Born free in New York, **Alexander Crummell** (1819–98) became an Episcopal priest in 1842. Several years later he went to England, where he earned a bachelor of arts degree at Queens' College, Cambridge University. Crummell went on to teach English and moral philosophy (ethics) at Liberia College in Liberia, West Africa, where he lived for twenty years. After he returned to the United States, settling in Washington, D.C., Crummell helped found an organization dedicated to advancing and promoting black scholarship: the American Negro Academy (1897).

trained physician in the United States, returned to New York City, the black community gave him a hero's welcome. He was feted on September 26, 1837, in Broadway Tabernacle's lecture hall. The man presiding over the event, Ransom F. Wake, reminded the crowd that Smith had been remarkable as a boy. Wake knew what he was talking about, for he had been one of Smith's teachers at African Free-School No. 2.

Before the year was out, Smith opened his practice in Lower Manhattan, at 93 West Broadway. He was on his way to becoming one of the city's preeminent physicians and pharmacists, caring for people no matter their race or ethnicity. (According to ads in the November 18, 1837, issue of New York's *Colored American*, the doctor was consulted on "Medical cures of every description" and his services included "Bleeding, Tooth-drawing, Cupping and Leeching.")

In 1846, Smith added to his practice by accepting the job of chief physician at the city's black orphanage. If that were not enough, Smith also tutored and counseled young men whose great ambitions were to be pharmacists or physicians.

When Smith wasn't healing or teaching people, this staunch abolitionist could be found serving on a committee of an antislavery organization or lecturing about the evils of slavery. An avid reader, he was also a prolific writer, churning out article after article for black- and white-owned newspapers, magazines, and journals: articles about medical matters, race matters, literature, the performing arts, and even chess. In 1855, Smith spent some of his time writing an introduction to *My Bondage and My Freedom*, the second autobiography of the equally famous abolitionist Frederick Douglass, whom he called his "brother."

And what did the great Frederick Douglass think of the doctor? In his third autobiography, while reflecting on those days when he was making his way in freedom after escaping slavery in 1838, Douglass ranked James McCune Smith as "foremost" among the "brave and intelligent" black men who gave him "their cordial sympathy and support."

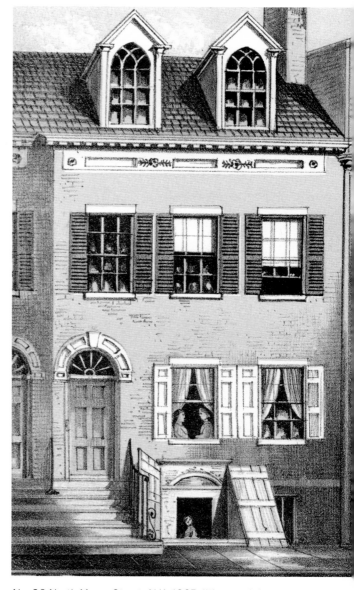

No. 86 North Moore Street, N.Y. 1865, lithograph by George Hayward. Dr. Smith had moved his family down the street to 15 North Moore Street in 1847. The house was several blocks north of his practice, by then at 55 West Broadway.

A FEMALE SPY.

Mary Bowser

c. 1841–?

On June 30, 1995, more than 150 years after her birth, Mary Bowser was inducted into the Military Intelligence Hall of Fame. She was described as "one of the highest-placed and most productive espionage agents of the Civil War."

This woman, whose life is shrouded in mystery, first appears in history on May 17, 1846. On that day, "Mary Jane, a colored child belonging to Mrs. Van Lew," was baptized at Saint John's Church in Richmond, Virginia, according to church records. Mrs. Van Lew, a white woman who lived in a mansion on Church Hill, was the widow of a wealthy hardware merchant.

OPPOSITE *A Female Spy*, engraving from Allan Pinkerton's book *The Spy of the Rebellion: Being a True History of the Spy System of the United States Army During the Late Rebellion* (1883). The woman depicted here is Washington, D.C., socialite Rose O'Neal Greenhow, one of the Confederacy's most famous spies. There are no known images of Mary Bowser.

The Confederate White House, at 1201 East Clay Street (1865), by an unidentified photographer.

missionary, the young woman returned to Richmond. This was in the winter of 1860, when tensions between the slave states and free states were running high. A year later came the Civil War, and Mary Bowser was soon in the thick of it, helping Elizabeth Van Lew help the Union.

Van Lew had been feeding information to the North for a while. After the Civil War broke out, her loyalty to the Union intensified. She expanded her network of pro-Union spies, tapping Mary Bowser to spy on Jefferson Davis, president of the Confederacy. Because Van Lew knew Davis's wife, Varina, she easily finessed a way to get Bowser hired as a servant in the Confederate White House, about a fifteen-minute walk from the Van Lew mansion.

Once in, Bowser played her part to the hilt—pretending to be an idiot. The politicians, military officers, and other whites who visited the Davises invariably regarded black people as ignorant, so they didn't have their guard up when Bowser was around. They spoke freely in the presence of this educated woman, who reportedly had a photographic memory and total recall of conversations.

As Bowser did things like wait at table, polish furniture and fireplace fixtures, and tidy President Davis's office, she stayed on the lookout for letters, reports—any

Though Mary began life as Van Lew property, by the time she was baptized, the little girl had been given her freedom and practically adopted by Mrs. Van Lew's daughter, Elizabeth—no ordinary Southern belle. This maverick sent Mary north to be educated in the late 1840s or early 1850s. In 1855, when Mary was about fifteen, she was packing her bags for New York. There, she boarded a ship bound for Liberia, West Africa, a nation founded by blacks from the States. After about four years as a

c. 1841
born Mary Richards in or near Richmond, Virginia.

April 16, 1861
marries Wilson Bowser, a Van Lew servant and also a spy.

c. early 1867
founds a school for blacks in Saint Marys, Georgia, having taught at other schools in the South.

c. June 27, 1867
last "sighted" in a letter informing a superior that she will soon leave Georgia, possibly for Cuba.

Elizabeth Van Lew (c. 1861), from the June 1911 *Harper's Monthly Magazine*.

IN HER TIME

On December 20, 1860, South Carolina seceded from the Union and called for a Confederate States of America. This was a month after Abraham Lincoln was elected president of the United States.

The Civil War started in South Carolina on April 12, 1861, when Confederate forces fired on Union-held Fort Sumter in Charleston Harbor. By then the confederation of slave states had seven members. By mid-June it had eleven.

Lincoln issued the Emancipation Proclamation on January 1, 1863. It declared that blacks enslaved in rebel-held territory were free. It also allowed black men to join the Union army.

The Civil War essentially ended on April 9, 1865, when the Confederacy's General Robert E. Lee surrendered in Virginia to Ulysses S. Grant, commander-in-chief of the Union army. Five days later Confederate sympathizer John Wilkes Booth shot President Lincoln, who died the following day.

information the Union could use. Whatever intelligence she gleaned from eavesdropping on conversations and riffling through papers she passed on to Elizabeth Van Lew. Van Lew then handed that information off to other agents, who relayed it to a member of the Union army.

Bowser sometimes slipped away to the Van Lew mansion to deliver intelligence personally. At other times she sewed dispatches into one of Mrs. Davis's gowns in need of repair, then dashed to a nearby seamstress, also in the spy network. This woman promptly signaled for Elizabeth Van Lew to stop by her shop.

The information Bowser dropped may have ranged from troop movements and supply routes to battle plans and changes in commands. "You have sent me the most valuable information received from Richmond," General Ulysses S. Grant told Elizabeth Van Lew after the war.

By then Mary Bowser was long gone from Richmond.

With Van Lew's help, she had been spirited out of the city in early 1865, after she learned that Jefferson Davis reckoned that there was a spy in his house. Bowser had reason to believe that she was the prime suspect.

On Sunday, September 10, 1865, five months after the war ended, the *New York Times* reported that on Monday evening at Abyssinian Baptist Church, then on Waverly Place, a Richmonia Richards, "connected with the secret service of our government," was to give a talk about her "adventures." Two days later, the *New York Tribune* reported that Miss Richards spoke of putting her life in peril "on many occasions." Few people doubt that this Richmonia Richards, aka Mary Richards aka Mary Jones aka Richmonia R. St. Pierre aka Mary J. R. Garvin, was Mary Bowser.

John Scobell (dates unknown): After his owner, a Confederate soldier, freed him at Manassas Junction, Virginia, Scobell made his way to a Union camp, where he was questioned about his former owner's regiment. The man asking the questions was Allan Pinkerton, chief of Union intelligence and founder of a detective agency in Chicago. After Scobell learned code, ways to conceal messages, and other spy craft, he became Secret Operative No. 6. Working mostly in Virginia, Scobell sometimes posed as a vendor, sometimes as a cook. When on a mission with white agents, he pretended to be their servant. Scobell, in turn, had spies of his own: fellow members of the Legal League, a black intelligence-gathering organization, also known as Lincoln's Legal Loyal League or the 4Ls. Their password was "For Light and Liberty."

President Lincoln Riding Through Richmond, April 4, amid the Enthusiastic Cheers of the Inhabitants, hand-colored engraving (based on a sketch by Joseph Becker), which originally appeared in the April 22, 1865, issue of *Frank Leslie's Illustrated Newspaper*. Shortly before Lincoln arrived in Richmond, Jefferson Davis fled the city and Union forces occupied it. In this illustration, Lincoln is on his way to the Confederate White House, which now served as the Union army's headquarters in Richmond. (Lincoln was assassinated a week before this appeared.)

TOWN
FOUNDER

Allen **Allensworth**

1842–1914

Twelve-year-old Allen saw tears streaming down his mother's face as he stood in her cabin. His mother lay in bed, utterly forlorn. Her husband had died a few years back. Her other twelve sons and daughters were long gone from Louisville, Kentucky. Some had been sold. Others had escaped. Now Allen, her youngest, was being taken from her.

The boy had been sold to a man with a plantation in Henderson County, Kentucky, more than one hundred miles away. The sale was Allen's punishment for trying to improve himself by honing his reading and writing skills.

OPPOSITE Allen Allensworth in the U.S. Army. Photograph (date unknown) by a Mr. Elrod of Louisville, Kentucky.

April 7, 1842
born in Louisville, Kentucky.

September 20, 1877
marries Josephine Leavell, a music teacher, with whom he will have two daughters.

September 14, 1914
dies in Monrovia, California.

THE PARTING "Buy us too."

Allen's mistress, Bett Starbird, had told him to stop that learning when she discovered that he had tricked her son, Tommy, into playing "school" with him. To put an end to it, she rented out Allen to do odd jobs for the mother of a local white merchant, Mr. Talbot. That plan backfired. Talbot's mother tutored the boy and let him attend a school for black children in a nearby church. When the Starbirds found out . . .

Allen looked on silently as his mother rose from her bed, "crept over to one corner of the room" where she kept a battered box, searched through it, then finally brought out a silver half dollar. "Take this, my son, buy yourself a book and a comb," she said. "Put knowledge from the book into your head and comb everything else out with the comb."

The boy was soon led from the cabin by Reuben, the Starbirds' coachman, who had fetched him from the Talbots to bid his mother farewell. On the way to the river, Reuben let the lad buy a comb, then a spelling book. In less than an hour Allen was aboard a steamer named *Rainbow*.

Allen had much to "comb out" in Henderson. For starters, his new mistress, Hebe Smith, confiscated his comb. Things got worse after she got wind of his reading and writing. Allen was subjected to "a series of persecutions to throttle every ambition, stifle every desire, and choke every aspiration that was within me to carry out the instructions of my mother to prepare myself to be a good and useful man."

The child was lashed on trumped-up charges. One time he was falsely accused of stealing cucumbers; another time, of stealing money. For that, "I was denuded, tied, bucked and gagged, and for three hours I was whipped unmercifully."

ABOVE *The Parting—Buy Us Too* (c. 1863), lithograph by James Queen based on an illustration by Henry Louis Stephens. This illustration of a family being broken up by sale captures the anguish young Allensworth and his mother felt when he was sold away.

OPPOSITE *View of the City of Louisville, Kentucky*, hand-colored engraving that originally appeared in the September 2, 1854, issue of *Gleason's Pictorial Drawing-Room Companion*.

No amount of terror and torture stopped Allen from striving to be the kind of person his mother wanted him to be—and the kind of person *he* wanted to be: a good and useful man. Not the punishments he suffered after several failed attempts to escape. Nor his sale to several other white men, the last of whom decided to train him to be a jockey. When this fellow sent the boy to his horse-racing camp near Louisville, Kentucky, Allen saw his mother again!

The Civil War broke out a few months after this reunion. Allen took advantage of the chaos to escape, and this time he succeeded. He then proceeded with the business of being a good and useful man.

Allen Allensworth served as a Union army nurse in Evansville, Indiana; Georgetown and Cincinnati, Ohio; and Mound City, Illinois. In the spring of 1863, he joined the Union navy, serving first as a seaman, then rising to a wardroom steward.

After the war Allensworth pressed on with his education, attending Ely Normal School in Louisville, Kentucky, then Baptist Theological Institute in Nashville, Tennessee, an ancestor of LeMoyne-Owen College in Memphis. In addition to pastoring several churches in

IN HIS TIME

Slavery was abolished in the United States when the Constitution's Thirteenth Amendment was ratified on December 6, 1865.

Blacks gained citizenship when the Constitution's Fourteenth Amendment was ratified on July 9, 1868.

Black men gained the right to the national vote when the Constitution's Fifteenth Amendment was ratified on February 3, 1870.

The Spanish-American War ended on December 10, 1898, with the signing of the Treaty of Paris. As a result of the war, Spain relinquished its claim on Cuba, gave the United States Guam and Puerto Rico, and agreed to let it buy the Philippines for $20 million. During the war, the Hawaiian islands became a U.S. territory.

Other Black Towns

Eatonville, Florida (1887)
This town, still very much alive, about six miles north of Orlando, is the hometown of anthropologist and writer Zora Neale Hurston, best known for *Their Eyes Were Watching God* (1937), a novel set in Eatonville.

Boley, Oklahoma (1903)
Its founders included Thomas M. Haynes, a black entrepreneur, and John Boley, a white railroad manager. Boley was one of more than fifty black towns founded in Oklahoma in the early 1900s and one of a handful that survived into the twenty-first century.

Mound Bayou, Mississippi (1887)
This town, still in existence, was the brainchild of Isaiah T. Montgomery and his cousin Benjamin Green, both born into slavery.

Kentucky, Allensworth became a star on the black lecture circuit. One of his most popular talks was "The Battle of Life and How to Fight It."

In 1886, Allen Allensworth returned to the U.S. army as a chaplain. He was assigned to the Twenty-Fourth Infantry Regiment, a black unit. As part of his ministry to these soldiers, Captain Allensworth operated schools for them and their families as they moved from post to post. Those posts included Fort Bayard in New Mexico and Fort Douglas in Utah. From there, in the summer of 1898, the Twenty-Fourth Infantry was deployed to Cuba, where it joined Colonel Teddy Roosevelt's Rough Riders in the Battle of San Juan Hill, the most famous battle of the Spanish-American War, which began in late April 1898.

Allen Allensworth retired from the U.S. army in April 1906 as a lieutenant colonel. He was the highest-ranking black officer and highest-ranking chaplain in the U.S. military when he returned to civilian life. He settled in Los Angeles, California.

Now in his sixties, he did one more good and useful thing. In the summer of 1908 he helped found the town of Allensworth, a place where blacks could be farmers, merchants, artisans, or anything else they wanted to be. Free of racial prejudice. Free of racist laws. Free of false assumptions about their abilities and intellects. Allensworth's town, located about forty miles north of Bakersfield, California, eventually became a ghost town, but while it existed, it was a real oasis. It was good. It was useful. The townsite became all that again when it was transformed into the Colonel Allensworth State Historic Park in 1974.

Charge of the 24th and 25th Colored Infantry and Rescue of Rough Riders at San Juan Hill, July 2nd, 1898 (1899), lithograph (water-damaged) by Kurz & Allison. The Ninth and Tenth Calvary, two more black units, were also in the fight—in the charge up nearby Kettle Hill. After the battles, which actually occurred on July 1, a white corporal told a reporter, "If it had not been for the Negro Cavalry the Rough Riders would have been exterminated." ("Rough Riders" was the nickname of the First U.S. Volunteer Cavalry under the command of Theodore Roosevelt, future U.S. president.)

Clara Brown

1800–1885

Ten years after the California forty-niners, another gold rush was on. This one was in Pikes Peak country, part of western Kansas and southwestern Nebraska territories at the time, in what is now Colorado.

Clara Brown, nearing sixty, was a witness to the 1859 Pikes Peak gold rush. Up for adventure and new vistas, Brown headed across the Great Plains that spring with a wagon train of about two dozen miners. She paid for her passage with her labor—nursing, cooking, doing laundry. Two dusty months and seven hundred miles later, she was in Cherry Creek, near Denver, then just a village. Clara Brown was more than fifteen hundred miles away from Virginia, where she was born into a life of hardship and pain.

OPPOSITE
Clara Brown (c. 1875–85), by Green & Concannon.

Crossing the Platte, an engraving based on a drawing by Albert Bierstadt from the August 13, 1859, issue of *Harper's Weekly*.

Clara was three years old when she and her mother were on the auction block in Spotsylvania County, Virginia, sold to a tobacco planter, then taken to his plantation in Logan County, Kentucky. Young Clara's father had been sold to somebody else.

She was in her twenties when one of her twin daughters, Paulina Ann, died in an accidental drowning.

She was in her thirties when, after that Logan County tobacco planter died, she and her husband, Richard; son, Richard Jr.; and remaining two daughters were auctioned off—husband and son to cotton planters in the Deep South, she and her daughters to different owners in Kentucky.

She was in her fifties when her third owner died and his daughters freed her.

By then she had heard that her daughter Margaret was dead.

Now that Brown had her freedom, foremost on her mind was finding her remaining daughter, Eliza Jane, the other twin. But time and the law were not on this mother's side. Free blacks couldn't live in Kentucky permanently. If Brown stayed in the state for more than a year, she could wind up on an auction block. Again.

Rather than risk re-enslavement, Clara Brown left Kentucky sometime in 1857, settling about three hundred miles northwest, in Saint Louis, Missouri. There, she worked as a cook for a German family, the Brunners. When they moved to Kansas Territory, Brown moved with them. When the family moved again, this time to California, Clara Brown stayed put and started a laundry business. A few years later came the "Pikes Peak or Bust" cavalcade, with Clara Brown ready to pull up stakes. When she did, she probably never gave it a thought that she might be one of the first, if not the first, black woman to set foot in what became Colorado.

After Clara Brown reached Cherry Creek in June 1859, she bought a one-room cabin. From it she ran a laundry business—and it

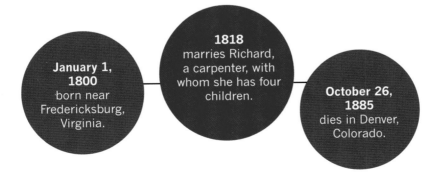

January 1, 1800
born near Fredericksburg, Virginia.

1818
marries Richard, a carpenter, with whom she has four children.

October 26, 1885
dies in Denver, Colorado.

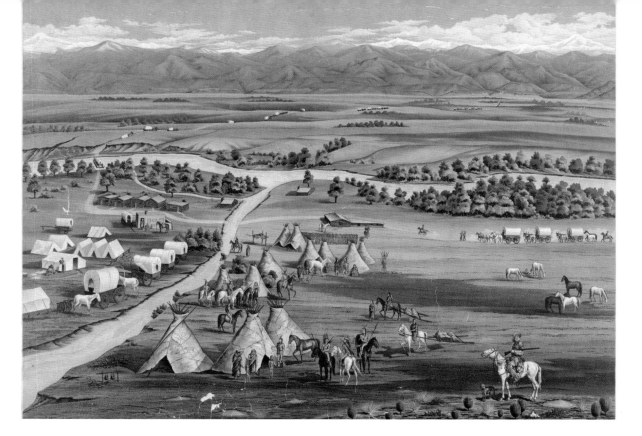

Denver in 1859 (c. April 21, 1891), lithograph by Collier & Cleveland Lithograph Company.

thrived, enabling her to invest in real estate. Seeking even brisker business, she eventually settled about forty miles west, in the mining camp of Central City. There, she made money hand over fist preparing grub along with doing laundry.

Clara Brown continued to work and invest in real estate. By the time the Civil War was over in 1865, she was worth around ten thousand dollars, which would be about $150,000 today. She would have been worth even more had she not made a large donation to the building fund for a black Methodist church and had she not fed and sheltered black and white miners and their families when they fell on hard times.

In 1866, with slavery abolished, Clara Brown, in her sixties, made tracks for Kentucky to search for her daughter, Eliza Jane, a search that was in vain. Ready to return to the West, Brown took pity on a group of destitute blacks she encountered, folks up for making a new start in Colorado Territory, organized back in 1861 out of pieces of Kansas, Nebraska, New Mexico, and Utah territories.

Brown paid for the whole kit and caboodle needed to get these sixteen people back West with her. Then she took care of them until they got on their feet. As a reporter later noted, she never tired of turning her home into "a hospital, a hotel, and general refuge for those who were sick or in poverty. If those who made her home their home were able to pay her for what they received, she accepted it; if not, it did not matter." There came a day when this woman called the "Angel of the Rockies," needed big help herself.

A native of Tennessee, the six-foot-tall, two-hundred-pound **Mary Fields** (c. 1832–1914) became a legend in Montana. She picked up the nickname "Stagecoach Mary" because for eight years she was a U.S. mail carrier—a job she started when she was about sixty years old! Fields's route was between Cascade and Saint Peter's Mission, about fifteen miles away. "She could use a four-horse lash with a dexterity that made a man green with envy, and she also could use a six-shooter with equal accuracy," said Montana's *Anaconda Standard* in April 1913 in an article about Stagecoach Mary's eighty-third birthday.

George Washington (1817–1905), born in Virginia to an enslaved black man and a white woman, was adopted as a baby by a white couple, James and Anna Cochran. The family moved to Ohio, then to Missouri, and finally to Oregon Territory, where George amassed several hundred acres of land. He also founded a town in 1875, known today as Centralia, Washington.

In 1874, several of Brown's properties, including her home, went up in flames in a fire that destroyed most of Central City. Her loss of property in the fire was not her first financial calamity. Before the war she had lost other property in a flood. Back in 1866, during her trip to Kentucky, she had been robbed of or swindled out of four thousand dollars. Despite these losses, Clara Brown had continued to be generous. As her funds dwindled, she did not stop helping people in need.

After the fire in 1874, a friend let Brown live in a cottage he owned. From there, she got back on her feet by returning to the laundry business. Several years later, another friend moved her into a cottage in Denver. Clara Brown, suffering heart trouble, probably figured that was the last journey she would make, but two years later wild horses couldn't stop her from making a six-hundred-mile trip to Council Bluffs, Iowa.

With donations from friends, Brown boarded a Union Pacific train in March 1882, bound for Omaha, Nebraska, where she transferred to a horse-drawn trolley that took her to Council Bluffs. That's where her daughter, Eliza Jane, a widow, was living, a friend had written. That friend was right! After nearly fifty years, Clara Brown at last could once again wrap her arms around one of her children—and a granddaughter, Cindy! And both were by her side when she died three years later.

On October 27, 1885, under the headline "Death of a Pioneer," Denver's *Rocky Mountain News* informed its readers that Clara Brown, in her eighties, "who has been lying at the point of death for several days at her home, 607 Arapahoe Street, died last evening at 8:30 o'clock." The Pioneer association was handling the funeral arrangements, the item said.

The "Pioneer association" was shorthand for the predominantly white Colorado Society of Pioneers, into which Clara Brown was inducted in 1882. She certainly fit the criteria: (1) she had arrived in Colorado before January 1, 1861, when it wasn't its own territory, and (2) she had been an asset to the state.

Ever since Clara Brown fell on hard times, the Pioneer association had been helping her out. It was the right and proper thing to do, given how much she had helped so many others over the years and given all that she had endured.

This mid-1860s photograph by an unidentified photographer looks north over Central City.

IN HER TIME

As a result of the Mexican-American War (1846–48), the United States became about 500,000 square miles larger. The land Mexico ceded became all or part of the following states: Arizona, California, Colorado, Nevada, New Mexico, Utah, and Wyoming.

The first transcontinental railroad was completed on May 10, 1869, at Promontory Summit, Utah, making east-west movement of people and freight easier and faster. At one point, on the route east from Sacramento to the California-Nevada border, about 80 percent of the labor force—and the men assigned the most dangerous work, such as dynamiting tunnels—were Chinese immigrants, who faced severe discrimination, including not being allowed to become U.S. citizens.

Having moved millions of Native Americans from the East in the early 1800s, starting in 1854 the U.S. government waged war on Arapahoe, Cheyenne, Comanche, Kiowa, Lakota, and other Native American tribes. It forced them onto reservations to make their land available to farmers, cattle ranchers, and others, as well as businesses.

Colorado became the thirty-eighth U.S. state on August 1, 1876.

CONCERT
SINGER

Sissieretta Jones

1868–1933

Sissieretta Jones had performed at New York City's Madison Square Garden and Carnegie Hall. Her voice had entranced music lovers in Jamaica, Barbados, Grenada, and other islands in the West Indies. She had even sung at the White House, for President Benjamin Harrison, in the Blue Room.

Now, in late 1894, this phenomenal soprano was to embark on a European tour. What a long way—a very long way—she had come!

Born in Virginia a few years after the end of the Civil War, Sissieretta Jones was the daughter of a couple born into slavery, a couple who split up when she was a child. By then Providence, Rhode Island, was home.

OPPOSITE
Sissieretta Jones
(date unknown),
by Addison
Scurlock.

One of the many medals Sissieretta Jones received during her career. The Society of the Sons of New York, a black fraternal organization, gave her this "Excelsior" medal when she made her debut at Carnegie Hall on June 15, 1892, sharing the bill with baritone Henry T. Burleigh and several other famous singers and musicians. The Sons of New York sponsored the concert to benefit the poor in their community. "Excelsior" is Latin for "higher."

Song was the girl's solace and source of joy early on. "I can never remember the time when I did not sing," she told the *San Francisco Call* in 1896. "I used to sing to myself as a child because I loved music."

Young Sissieretta sang at home, in church, in school. She sang year after year, but she didn't have professional training until she was a teenager. With whom she studied voice and music then and later is a bit sketchy. In any event, over the years, Sissieretta continued to sing in church concerts and with amateur bands. In May 1885, at Providence's Armory Hall, she shared the stage with Flora Batson, an already established black concert singer.

Sissieretta Jones was soon a sensation in New England, then elsewhere in the nation. Her repertoire ranged from folk songs like the Scottish "Comin' Thro' the Rye" to operatic works, such as "Caro Nome" from Giuseppe Verdi's *Rigoletto* and an aria from Giacomo Meyerbeer's *L'Africaine*. In her silk, satin, and velvet gowns, Jones looked as exquisite as she sounded. Her earnings were fabulous, too. When she set sail for Europe in 1895, she was one of the highest-paid black entertainers in the States—she was grossing about eight thousand dollars a year. At the time, many Americans earned nearer to four hundred dollars a year.

Sissieretta Jones's nine-month European tour included performances in London, Paris, and several German cities.

"Her voice is clear and true up to the highest tones," said a German critic who attended Jones's concert at Berlin's Wintergarten theater on February 19, 1895, the start of her tour.

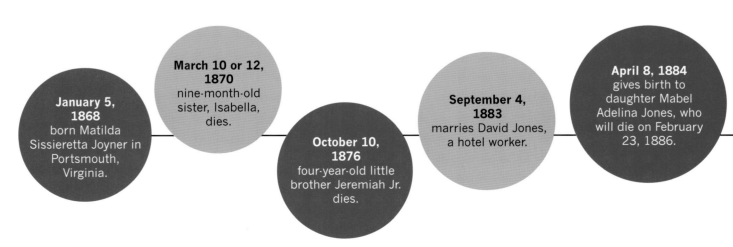

January 5, 1868
born Matilda Sissieretta Joyner in Portsmouth, Virginia.

March 10 or 12, 1870
nine-month-old sister, Isabella, dies.

October 10, 1876
four-year-old little brother Jeremiah Jr. dies.

September 4, 1883
marries David Jones, a hotel worker.

April 8, 1884
gives birth to daughter Mabel Adelina Jones, who will die on February 23, 1886.

The Black Patti, Mme. M. Sissieretta Jones the Greatest Singer of Her Race (1899), created by Metropolitan Printing Company in New York. People called Jones "the Black Patti," comparing her to a contemporary: the world-famous Italian opera singer Adelina Patti (1843–1919).

On May 18, 1896, the U.S. Supreme Court handed down its decision in the case known as *Plessy v. Ferguson*, ruling that maintaining separate but "equal" facilities, from playgrounds and movie theaters to schools, for whites and people of color was constitutional. Local and state Jim Crow laws and customs already existed. After the *Plessy* decision, they increased and were more rigorously enforced.

In 1910, about 90 percent of blacks in the United States lived in the South. By 1916, a great exodus was under way, with blacks seeking better-paying jobs, better housing, and less racial oppression. Millions left cities such as Bessemer, Alabama; Gulfport, Mississippi; New Orleans; and Houston for West Coast cities like Los Angeles, Midwestern cities like Chicago and Detroit, and, in the Northeast, cities like New York and Philadelphia. This Great Migration lasted for decades.

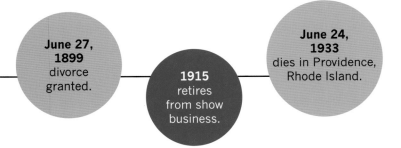

June 27, 1899 divorce granted.

1915 retires from show business.

June 24, 1933 dies in Providence, Rhode Island.

"The applause which greeted the close of each number," reported Berlin's *Börsen-Courier*, "was a tribute to a talent which is quite independent of color or nationality, a talent worthy of admiration for its own sake alone."

Germany's emperor, Wilhelm II, was among the notables who saw Jones perform in Berlin. He reportedly had a diamond cross made for her as a show of appreciation. Later, when Jones made her London debut, Albert Edward, the Prince of Wales (the future King Edward VII of England), was in the audience.

Sissieretta Jones had been back in the States about six months when a reporter with the *San Francisco Call* interviewed her in her rooms at a swanky hotel, the Russ House, in July 1896. Her answer when asked if she wanted to perform onstage in operas—yes! She most certainly did! But Jones didn't think this dream would come true because she traveled so much. Besides, she couldn't see a white opera company opening its doors to a black artist. (At the time, there were no black opera companies.)

Pressing the matter further, the reporter suggested that with clever application of makeup and wigs, she might be able to get into an opera company by pretending to be white. Sissieretta Jones balked at that. "Try to hide my race and deny my own people? Oh, I would never do that." After a pause, she added, "I am proud of belonging to them and would not hide what I am even for an evening."

OPPOSITE With the growing popularity of vaudeville, in 1897 Sissieretta Jones formed her own troupe of singers, dancers, and comics.

Songs AS SUNG BY THE BLACK PATTI Troubadours

THE GREATEST Colored Show ON EARTH.

VOEICKEL & NOLAN
PROPRIETORS & MANAGERS.

WORDS & MUSIC
PRICE 25 CENTS.

PUBLISHED BY
M. WITMARK & SONS.
NEW YORK — CHICAGO.

M. SISSIERETTA JONES
(BLACK PATTI)

BANK
FOUNDER

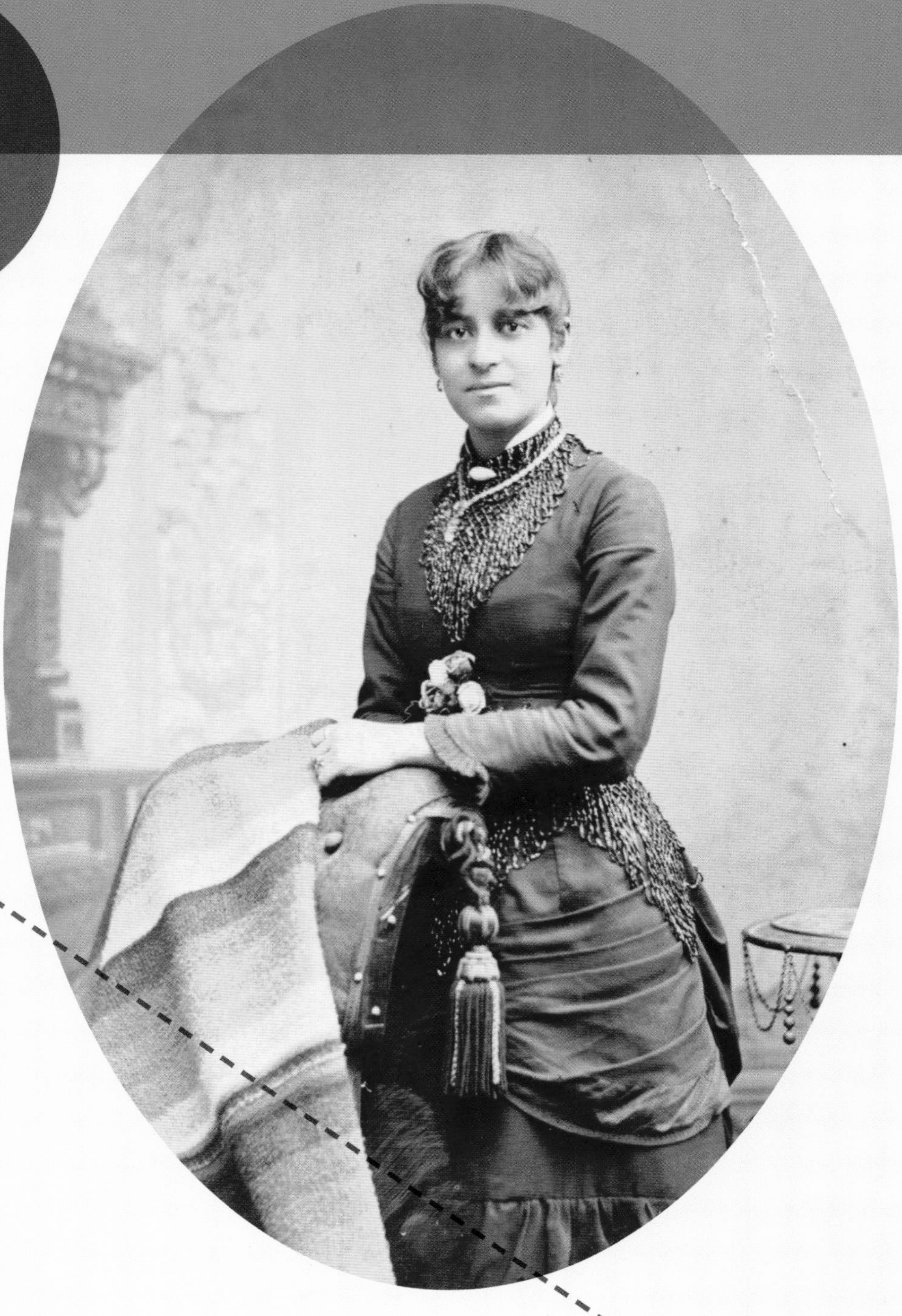

Maggie Lena Walker

1864–1934

There were about twenty black-owned banks in the United States when Maggie Lena Walker issued a call for another one. She did this on August 20, 1901, at the annual convention of the Independent Order of Saint Luke, the charitable organization she headed. "Let us put our moneys together," Walker urged; "let us use our moneys; let us put our money out at usury among ourselves, and reap the benefit ourselves. Let us have a bank that will take the nickels and turn them into dollars."

Two years later, on November 2, 1903, the Saint Luke Penny Savings Bank was open for business in Richmond, Virginia. The visionary Maggie Lena Walker was at the helm—and making history as the first black woman to run a bank.

OPPOSITE
Maggie Lena Walker in her twenties (c. 1885), by an unidentified photographer.

On its first day of business, the Saint Luke Penny Savings Bank had nearly three hundred customers. Between those who opened accounts with as little as thirty-one cents and those who did so with a hundred dollars or more, at day's end the bank had about eight thousand dollars in its vault. Not bad, considering that its president never went to business school. But that's not to say that Maggie Lena Walker didn't do her level best to prepare herself for the job. From the time of her appointment on August 21, 1903, until the bank opened some ten weeks later, Walker learned everything she could about banking by spending two hours a day, Monday through Friday, at the Merchants National Bank of Richmond. This was a white-owned bank whose founder, John P. Branch, was known for kindnesses toward blacks.

What Walker lacked in formal business education she more than made up for with a willingness to work hard, think hard—plus an aptitude for turning can't into can! And she, born free on the same Van Lew estate as the Union spy Mary Bowser, was in the habit of doing all this when young. As she famously said, "I was not born with a silver spoon in my mouth, but with a laundry basket practically on my head."

At the age of twelve, Maggie was working in her mother's home-based laundry business on College Alley in Richmond, Virginia. Fetching water, scrubbing collars, ironing, and making pickups and deliveries were some of the girl's tasks. Could young Maggie do all this *and* her regular household chores *and* keep up with her schoolwork? Yes, most definitely this girl could—and did, from her days in elementary school through her studies at a teacher-training institute, Richmond Colored Normal School. She graduated from the institute in 1883.

While doing all this, young Maggie was rising in an organization founded in 1867 by a black woman in Baltimore, Maryland. Originally named the Daughters of Saint Luke, it became the Independent Order of Saint Luke when men were allowed membership. The order provided its dues-paying members with burial insurance policies. It also came to people's aid with goods, money, and comfort in times of illness or unemployment.

Walker joined the order at fourteen. At fifteen, she was secretary of its Good Idea Council No. 16. At sixteen, she was a delegate to its annual convention in Petersburg, Virginia. She remained active with the order after she became a teacher,

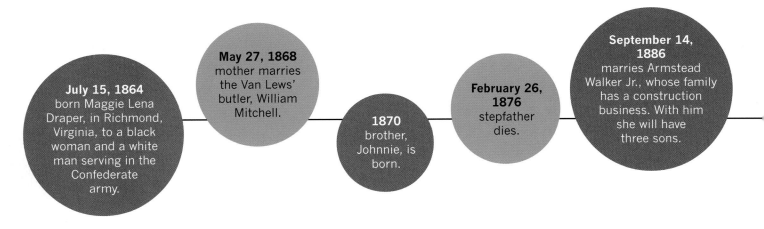

July 15, 1864
born Maggie Lena Draper, in Richmond, Virginia, to a black woman and a white man serving in the Confederate army.

May 27, 1868
mother marries the Van Lews' butler, William Mitchell.

1870
brother, Johnnie, is born.

February 26, 1876
stepfather dies.

September 14, 1886
marries Armstead Walker Jr., whose family has a construction business. With him she will have three sons.

then stepped up her commitment to it in 1895 by creating a Juvenile Department. Its mission: to instill in children the importance of education, self-sufficiency, and right living. "As the twig is bent, the tree is inclined" was the youth division's motto. A few years later, Walker was the order's executive director.

When Maggie Lena Walker became the order's chief in 1899—officially its "Right Worthy Grand Secretary"—it was no plum position. Membership was down, and so were the order's funds. While many people thought the order couldn't go on, Maggie Lena Walker thought, *Can!*

She mounted a massive membership drive. She gave speeches in churches, in meeting halls, in schools. In time, this powerhouse had the order in right worthy

Walker's concern for children was long-lasting. In this c. 1917 photograph, possibly taken by George O. Brown, she posed with children from Jackson Ward, the heart of black Richmond. It's where Walker and her family lived, in a townhouse at 110½ East Leigh Street, renovated over the years from nine to twenty-eight rooms.

February 4, 1894
middle son, seven-month-old Armstead, dies.

April 23, 1894
brother dies.

June 20, 1915
oldest son, Russell, fatally shoots his father, mistaking him for a burglar.

November 23, 1923
son Russell dies.

December 15, 1934
dies in Richmond, Virginia.

The first U.S. black-owned bank to open its doors did so in Washington, D.C., in October 1888: the Capital Savings Bank. On the eve of the Great Depression there were twenty-one black-owned banks in the nation. Only six survived the economic collapse.

In 1896, two black women's self-help and civil rights organizations merged to form the National Association of Colored Women's Clubs (NACWC). The NACWC's motto was "Lifting as We Climb." Its founders included Harriet Tubman and journalist and anti-lynching crusader Ida B. Wells-Barnett. The NACWC's first president was Mary Church Terrell, who had taught foreign languages at the M Street High School of Washington, D.C., one of the nation's most rigorous schools.

The National Association for the Advancement of Colored People (NAACP) was formed in February 1909. Its founders included white suffragist and journalist Mary White Ovington, white journalist Oswald Garrison Villard (a grandson of abolitionist William Lloyd Garrison), and W.E.B. Du Bois, the first black person to earn a PhD from Harvard University (1895). Maggie Lena Walker cofounded the NAACP's Richmond branch.

In 1916, the white suffragist Alice Paul formed the National Woman's Party (NWP). Its mission: to secure the national vote for women and passage of the Equal Rights Amendment.

American women gained the right to the national vote when the Constitution's Nineteenth Amendment was ratified on August 18, 1920.

shape. In January 1902, at the Saint Luke Hall, a three-story brick building at 900 Saint James Street, Walker launched a weekly newspaper, the *Saint Luke Herald*, trumpeting news and other information important to the black community. The newspaper also increased the order's visibility. Higher visibility meant more members, which under Walker's leadership would rise to more than 100,000, with chapters in more than twenty states and Washington, D.C. The *Saint Luke Herald* also promoted the Saint Luke Penny Savings Bank, which Walker, a wife and mother, continued to head for years.

Like the *Saint Luke Herald*, the Saint Luke Penny Savings Bank created jobs for black people. So, too, did the Saint Luke Emporium, a department store the order opened in 1905 at 112 Broad Street, now also the bank's home. The store was not as profitable as Walker had hoped, and she closed it in 1911. By then the bank was no longer part of the order but a separate entity renamed the Saint Luke Bank and Trust Company.

Walker's bank held on when hard times hit. While thousands of U.S. banks went bust after the October 1929 stock market crash, Walker kept hers going by merging with two other black-owned banks in Richmond. This new bank, the Consolidated Bank and Trust, opened for business on January 2, 1930. And Maggie Lena Walker was still thinking, *Can!* Though confined to a wheelchair due to complications of diabetes, she was the new bank's chairman of the board, a bank that thrived until 2009.

Another Who Could (and Did!)

Born in Metropolis, Illinois, to poor farmers, **Annie Turnbo Malone** (1869–1957) had a net worth of $14 million by 1930. She made her money in Saint Louis, Missouri, as CEO of a business that specialized in beauty products for black women. Malone named her company Poro, derived from a West African word that means physical and spiritual growth. By the mid-1920s Malone had about 75,000 agents in the United States and the Caribbean. Her headquarters was a building that took up a city block in the black section of Saint Louis known as the Ville. Here Malone employed more than 150 people in her beauty college, factory, labs, barbershop, cafeteria, and ice cream shop. One of Malone's early students and sales representatives was Sarah Breedlove, who also made millions in the beauty business under the name Madam C. J. Walker.

Seen here in this c. 1911–29 postcard is the final headquarters of Walker's bank. It moved into this building on First and Marshall Streets in 1911.

RACE CAR DRIVER

CHARLES WIGGINS
Winner of the 100 Mile Auto Race
Indianapolis, Aug. 7, 1926

Charlie **Wiggins**

1897–1979

"This auto race will be recognized throughout the length and breadth of the land as the single greatest sports event to be staged annually by colored people." That was sportswriter Frank A. Young in the *Chicago Defender*. The date: July 5, 1924.

Young was writing about the upcoming hundred-mile race at the Indiana State Fairgrounds in Indianapolis. "Soon, chocolate jockeys will mount their gas-snorting, rubber-shod Speedway monsters as they race at death-defying speeds . . . and the greatest array of driving talent will be in attendance in hopes of winning gold for themselves and glory for their Race." Without meaning to, Young gave William Rucker the perfect name for the event: the Gold and Glory Sweepstakes.

OPPOSITE
Wiggins with his 1926 Gold and Glory trophy, by an unidentified photographer.

Greel's Shoe-shining Parlor, Indianapolis, Ind. Said he was 15 years old. Works some nights until 11. Taken at 10 P.M. Location: Indianapolis, Indiana (1908), by Lewis Hine.

William Rucker was the black man promoting the event. The one who inspired it was "Wee" Charlie Wiggins. "Wee" because he was slim, small boned, and not that tall. But there was nothing at all "wee" about Wiggins's spirit.

Born in horse-and-buggy days on the cusp of the twentieth century, Charlie Wiggins grew up in the hardscrabble river town of Evansville, Indiana. He was working at age nine. After school, off he went to the coal mine (where his pa worked) to hustle up five-cent shoeshine jobs from the boss men. In time, Charlie was playing hooky from school. Instead of learning, he was earning money on Main and Eleventh Streets with his shoeshine kit. The kid made about a buck a day. With that dollar he could have bought a sirloin steak (a luxury for him) and still had change.

More than money, young Wiggins loved cars. Lucky for him, two of his regular customers were car dealers Henry Benninghoff and Eugene Nolan, and they had a garage a stone's throw away from Charlie's spot. During one shine, Charlie told these white men how crazy he was about cars.

Charlie soon became a regular at the garage. He went from watching mechanics

July 15, 1897
born Charles Edwin Wiggins in Evansville, Indiana, the oldest of his parents' three sons.

August 5, 1906
mother dies.

August 27, 1914
marries Roberta Sullinger, a former model, with whom he will have three boys, all of whom will die before turning one. After the couple moves to Indianapolis, Roberta becomes pregnant again, only to have a miscarriage.

March 11, 1979
dies in Indianapolis, Indiana.

make repairs to earning pocket change by washing cars and doing other odd jobs. A quick learner, he had just the right stuff to be a mechanic.

"He could just tell by the sound," a niece remembered. She was recalling the day Charlie was talking with Mr. Benninghoff when they suddenly heard a troubled car coming their way. Sight unseen, Charlie diagnosed the problem, judging only by the sound. Sure enough, when the mechanics got under the hood, they found that Charlie had nailed it.

In the summer of 1914, seventeen-year-old Charlie Wiggins became a mechanic apprentice at the Benninghoff-Nolan garage. He fetched things. He toted things. He was sometimes sent to junkyards to scavenge for spare parts. That was his day job. At night, he worked as a railroad porter.

After the United States entered World War I in April 1917, Wiggins wound up holding down the fort at the Benninghoff-Nolan garage as, one by one, the white mechanics joined the armed forces. (When Wiggins went to the recruiting station to enlist, he was given the brush-off and told, "This is a white man's war.")

While other men were stateside training or overseas fighting, Wiggins was becoming a matchless mechanic. Then, in the summer of 1922, he moved about two hundred miles north to Indianapolis, landing a job as a mechanic in this car lovers' paradise.

When it came to automobile manufacturing, Indianapolis rivaled Detroit, Michigan, as a motor city, producing a lot of high-end cars, like the Duesenberg. What's more, the city was home to the Indianapolis Motor Speedway, which held its first five-hundred-mile race in 1911.

On the Duesenberg factory floor (c. 1922), by an unidentified photographer. *Left:* The engine assembly area. *Right:* The assembly area for the Model A Dusenberg chassis. The brothers Fred and August Duesenberg, who came to the United States from Germany as children, opened their car plant on Indianapolis's West Washington Street in 1921, a year before Wiggins moved to the city.

GOLD and GLORY SWEEPSTAKES

UNDER NEW MANAGEMENT

100 MILE

ALL COLORED RACE DRIVERS

AUTO RACE

STATE FAIR GROUNDS

INDIANAPOLIS, INDIANA

Sunday, Sept. 20th

$1.00   *General Admission Plus 10c Tax*   **$1.00**

Charlie Wiggins would have given anything to enter the Indy 500, but racial prejudice prevented this. That didn't stop him from dreaming—so much so that he built a race car in the garage where he worked. He did it on his own time. He did it with a heap of parts from junkyards. When done, he named his race car the 23 Skidoo Wiggins Special.

"He just wouldn't give up," his wife, Roberta, remembered. "Race after race, he kept on entering his car. And race after race, they kept turning him away. But he was proving a point. He was exposing their prejudice. The white drivers all liked Charlie, but those promoters would have nothing to do with him."

Repeated rejection got black folks talking, then acting. With several other black men, William Rucker established a car racing league: the Colored Speedway Association (CSA). The CSA planned to sponsor races in various cities. The Gold and Glory Sweepstakes would be its annual crowning event.

About twelve thousand black people, most dressed to the nines, were in the stands for the first Gold and Glory Sweepstakes on August 2, 1924. The twenty-eight racers included "Cowboy" Moore from Chicago, driving his four-cylinder Dreamland Duesenberg; Jack "Long Shot" Sargent from Saint Louis, with his six-cylinder Shield Special; and Malcolm Hannon, a local, who won the first-place prize of $1,200. Hannon averaged 63.5 mph in his four-cylinder Barber-Warnock Ford.

Charlie Wiggins sat out the first Gold and Glory Sweepstakes race. This perfectionist didn't have the Wiggins Special as precisely tuned and calibrated as he wanted it. But he was ready for the next race and the next and the next . . .

Charlie Wiggins came in fifth in 1925, but he did much better in future races, coming in first in 1926, 1931, 1932, and 1933. (The Gold and Glory Sweepstakes was not held in 1934 and 1935.)

As Sunday, September 20, 1936, neared, the odds were that Wiggins would be the first-place winner in that year's Sweepstakes. "Black and white

IN HIS TIME

When Michigan automobile maker Henry Ford introduced the Model T on October 1, 1908, he shook up the car industry. Instead of catering to the wealthy with a car that cost thousands of dollars, Ford captured the attention of middle-income people with a car that cost $850 (equivalent to about $22,000 today). Ford went on to produce even more affordable Model Ts by making brilliant use of the assembly line. By 1920, one out of every two cars on the road was a Model T, costing about $400.

After World War I, with millions of American men back stateside and searching for jobs, in the spring, summer, and fall of 1919, the nation was a bloody mess. Whites started race riots in Charleston, South Carolina; Monticello, Mississippi; Bisbee, Arizona; Washington, D.C.; Chicago, Illinois; and about twenty-five other cities. Because the bloodiest riots occurred in the summer, this awful chapter in U.S. history became known as Red Summer.

Evansville, Indiana, became the headquarters of the Indiana branch of the recently revived Ku Klux Klan in 1920.

OPPOSITE An ad for the Gold and Glory Sweepstakes from the August 29, 1936, issue of the *Indianapolis Recorder*. This black-owned weekly began publication in 1895.

Born in Indianapolis, **Marshall Walter "Major" Taylor** (1878–1932) was one of the fastest cyclists of his day. He was world champion in the hundred-mile track race in 1899, 1900, and 1901. During all his years of physical training, Taylor worked hard to keep his character in good shape, too. His "A Dozen Don'ts" included "Don't get a swelled head" and "Don't forget to play the game fair."

drivers agree that Wiggins is one of the best race drivers Indianapolis has ever produced," said one article.

The 1936 Gold and Glory Sweepstakes was delayed first by a thundershower, then by a debate over the viability of one entrant's car. As the clock ticked, the worries mounted. State law mandated that all businesses and events be over and done with by five p.m. on Sundays. With time running out, the race finally started at 4:10 p.m., but without proper maintenance of the dirt track. It needed to be oiled and watered close to the time the race began, to cut down on the amount of dust the cars kicked up.

The track was soon so dusty that "you couldn't see ten feet in front of you," recalled one contestant. He and twenty-five other racers were still in the midst of the second lap when a car skidded and spun out of control.

In less than a minute, the Wiggins Special, going at about 80 mph—

"My God! My Charlie! My God!" Wiggins's wife screamed as she hurried over to a nightmare: a thirteen-car pileup. It was horrible, with vehicles "melting into a mountain of rending, distorted metal and buried men," reported the *Indianapolis Recorder*.

Miraculously, no one died on the track, but there were injuries—serious injuries in Wiggins's case. He was rushed to a hospital, where doctors saved his life but not his right leg. It had to be amputated.

After he recuperated, Charlie Wiggins didn't bow out of his beloved sport. No longer able to compete, this man called the "Negro Speed King" did the next best thing. He coached younger men who had a need for speed.

Firefighters along with drivers and mechanics work to extinguish the blaze in one of the thirteen cars that crashed during the 1936 Gold and Glory Sweepstakes. Photographer unknown.

Eugene **Bullard**

1895–1961

"I wasn't quite sure where that boat was heading but it was going to a place I had never seen before and that was good enough for me." That's what Eugene Bullard told a reporter in 1959. "That boat" was the cargo ship *Marta Russ*, and the year was 1912.

This was five years after Bullard, a native of Columbus, Georgia, sold his goat for a buck and a half and ran away from home. He was about eleven years old and craving adventure. He was also traumatized by his dad's almost getting lynched by a mob of drunken white men who had found out that Mr. Bullard had walloped a white man in self-defense. Young Eugene took off shortly after this incident.

October 9, 1895
born Eugene James Bullard in Columbus, Georgia, the seventh of his parents' ten children (three of whom died in infancy).

August 24, 1902
mother dies.

July 17, 1923
marries a white Frenchwoman from a wealthy family, Marcelle Straumann, with whom he will have three children, only two of whom will live into adulthood.

December 5, 1935
he and his wife divorce.

Summer 1940
arranges for his and his daughters' escape from Nazi-occupied France and their separate voyages to the United States.

October 12, 1961
dies in New York City.

During the boy's journey to no place in particular, he found angels along the way. There was Mary Woods of Atlanta, a black woman who put him up for a night. There was a band of Romani—commonly called Gypsies back then—who hailed from England. During Eugene's stay at their camp in Bronwood, Georgia, he learned how to race horses. Other angels included the Turners, a white family in Dawson, Georgia. They took the kid on as a stable boy and jockey in county fair races.

The young vagabond continued to knock about the South until in Norfolk, Virginia, he stowed away on the *Marta Russ*. Destination: Hamburg, Germany. Eugene was now sixteen.

After three days at sea the stowaway gave himself up to the ship's captain and soon found himself earning his keep by working in the boiler room, learning a bit of German in the process. That lasted until a few weeks later when the captain gave the young man five pounds and the heave-ho on the shores of Aberdeen, Scotland. There, Eugene hopped a train to Glasgow. About five months later he headed for Liverpool, England.

Dockworker, fishmonger, member of a vaudeville troupe doing slapstick— Eugene took on whatever work he could find in Liverpool. He spent some of his free time getting boxing lessons and even entered a few amateur bouts. He became a more skilled pugilist after he fell in with black American boxer Aaron Lester "Dixie Kid" Brown and followed him back to his base in London. The Dixie Kid, a welterweight, was like a father to Eugene.

Boxing matches took Bullard to Paris in late 1913, and the trip changed his life—he said he "could never be happy for the rest of my life unless I could live in France." Finally, he had found a place that called to him. He wound up settling in the City of Lights—soon a city in panic.

The assassinations of Austria's Archduke Franz Ferdinand and his wife, Duchess Sophie, in June 1914 triggered a chain reaction that led to

World War I. In this "Great War," the Central Powers, which included the Austrian-Hungarian Empire, Germany, and the Ottoman Empire, battled the Allied Powers, which included Great Britain, France, and eventually the United States.

Bullard, nineteen, was eager to fight for his adopted country. In early October 1914, he joined the French Foreign Legion. About a year later, because his Foreign Legion unit had been decimated, he was transferred to the French army's 170th Infantry, known as the "Swallows of Death."

Bullard saw action on the western front, first as a foot soldier and then as a machine gunner, cheating death through the Battle of Champagne, the Battle of the Somme, the Battle of Verdun; through the trenches, the stench, the barbed wire, the strafing, the shelling, the mud, and the blood and body parts of friends and foes. Bullard likened one of the casualties of the Battle of Verdun, the bombed-out village of Fleury, to a "Chicago slaughter house." Some of the blood that flowed in Fleury was his.

One day Bullard lost almost all his teeth when a shell exploded near him. A few days later, while he was trying to deliver a message from one French officer to another, a piece of shrapnel cut a hole in his thigh. For his gallantry the French government awarded Bullard a medal called the Croix de Guerre (Cross of War). The ceremony was held in June 1916, in Lyon, where he spent six months recuperating and getting dentures. Although Bullard's leg wound healed well, he was no longer fit to be a foot soldier. That, however, didn't stop him from getting back into the action.

After some seven months of training, he became an aircraft gunner in the French air force's Lafayette Flying Corps, an all-American volunteer outfit. Before long, Bullard, by now a corporal, set his sights higher. He yearned to be in the cockpit.

The wingover, the corkscrew dive, and the zoom are some of the maneuvers Bullard mastered to become the first black combat pilot in the world. He earned his wings in early May 1917, twenty-four years before the first Tuskegee Airmen took flight.

Ghastly Mementos of Battle at Verdun—Pile of Human Bones (c. 1933), by an unidentified photographer. After World War I, skeletal remains were gathered up, then laid to rest in an ossuary, or bone depository. An estimated 300,000 people died in the Battle of Verdun, which was fought from February 21 to December 18, 1916. Bullard was seriously wounded at Verdun.

LEFT Bullard in August or September 1917, by an unidentified photographer. The foot soldier turned pilot is standing beside a Nieuport 24 fighter, atop which sits Bullard's "copilot," his pet monkey Jimmy. He flew his first combat mission with Jimmy tucked in his jacket for good luck.

OPPOSITE This early-1900s postcard features one of Paris's most famous nightclubs, the Moulin Rouge (the Red Mill), home of the cancan dance. Bullard had a club near it.

38. ~ PARIS. ~ Le Moulin Rouge

PROMENOIR 2

With the publication of his collection of short stories *Tales of the Jazz Age* in 1922, F. Scott Fitzgerald coined the term "the Jazz Age" to describe an era of risk-taking and wild living, of hot jazz music and fast dancing, also known as "the Roaring Twenties" and "the Golden Twenties." The era, which really kicked off with the end of World War I in 1918, lasted until the bubble burst with the stock market crash in 1929. In the 1920s, jazz was all the rage in Paris, too.

On May 20, 1932, Amelia Earhart became the first woman to pull off a solo transatlantic flight. Earhart touched down in Londonderry, Northern Ireland, about fifteen hours after takeoff from Harbour Grace, Newfoundland, Canada.

On January 6, 1941, the U.S. War Department (later merged into today's Department of Defense) announced that a black pursuit (fighter) squadron was going to be trained in Tuskegee, Alabama. When World War II ended in 1945, about one thousand black men had been trained at Tuskegee's Moton Field. Tuskegee Airmen formed the 477th Medium Bombardment, which never saw action overseas, and the 332nd Pursuit Group (four fighter squadrons), which saw action escorting U.S. bombers in Germany, Italy, and North Africa.

Japanese pilots pulled off a devastating attack on the U.S. naval base at Pearl Harbor near Honolulu, Hawaii, on December 7, 1941. After this attack the United States entered World War II. The war ended after U.S. Army Air Corps pilots dropped atomic bombs on two Japanese cities, Hiroshima and Nagasaki, in August 1945.

When World War I ended in November 1918, Bullard had flown on twenty missions and was credited with shooting down at least one enemy plane, possibly a German Pfalz. Legend has it that he painted a bleeding heart on the fuselage of his airplane and below it wrote, *"Tout le Sang qui coule est rouge!"* (All blood runs red!).

After the war, Bullard stayed in France. He owned a nightclub in Paris, Le Grand Duc, at 52 rue Pigalle, where the young Langston Hughes was a dishwasher during his six-month visit in 1924. For a time, the black American jazz great Ada "Bricktop" Smith headlined at Le Grand Duc, a favorite haunt of F. Scott Fitzgerald, Pablo Picasso, and other artists and intellectuals. Bullard, who gave himself the middle name Jacques, was having the time of his life in France, where blacks generally experienced less racism than they did in the States. He probably would have spent the rest of his life in France, had it not been for the Nazis.

Some Other Early Flyboys

Born in Canton, Oklahoma, **James Herman Banning** (1899–1933) learned to fly in Des Moines, Iowa, when he attended Iowa State College for about a year. In 1932, pilot Banning and mechanic Thomas C. Allen became the first blacks to make a coast-to-coast flight when they took off from Los Angeles, California, on September 18 and landed on Long Island, New York, on October 9. Clearly it was not a nonstop flight. Their forty-two hours in the air spanned twenty-one days because the daring duo periodically touched down to refuel their Alexander Eaglerock biplane and to raise money for the next leg of the journey.

Trinidadian **Hubert Fauntleroy Julian** (1897–1983) came to the States in 1921 by way of Canada, where he had learned to fly. This flamboyant man, who spoke French and Italian, made a name for himself doing parachute jumps and other stunts in air shows.

A native of Henderson, Kentucky, who spent most of his early life in Chicago, **William J. Powell** (1897–1942) started a flying club in Los Angeles in 1931 to boost black interest in aviation and aeronautics. He named his club after Bessie Coleman, the first black woman to get her wings (1922). On Labor Day 1931, Powell's Bessie Coleman Aero Club sponsored the first black air show.

Germany occupied France in June 1940, about nine months after the outbreak of World War II. Great Britain, France, the Soviet Union, and eventually the United States were among the Allied Powers that went up against Germany, Italy, and Japan, the Axis Powers.

France was no longer a safe place to be if you were black. Nazis hated black people as much as they hated Jews, gays, and Romani. Still, Bullard didn't jump ship. Not at first. Not until he had served a brief stint as a machine gunner with the French resistance and was again severely wounded. After more than twenty years in France, this man with nine lives and a million stories to tell made his way back to the United States via Spain and Portugal.

Eugene Bullard stayed in the States for the rest of his days, living in New York City's Spanish Harlem. He worked a variety of jobs (dockworker, security guard, elevator operator) and spent much of his free time with French émigrés. In the fall of 1959, the sixty-four-year-old veteran of French armed forces was made a Knight of the Legion of Honor, France's highest honor for distinguished service. This was the fifteenth honor France bestowed upon Bullard. This braveheart was nearly done with his memoir when he died two years later. Its title: *All Blood Runs Red: My Adventurous Life in Search of Freedom*.

Bullard (c. 1917, by an unidentified photographer) with comrades from the French army's 170th Infantry, in which he served after his stint with the French Foreign Legion and then again after he was booted out of France's air force in November 1917. Bullard believed that a white American military officer was responsible for this. Earlier, when Bullard tried to join the American air force, he was rejected.

FILMMAKER

Oscar **Micheaux**

1884–1951

Foundryman, coal miner, steelworker, shoeshine boy, Pullman porter—by the time Oscar Micheaux was twenty-one, he had been all those things. Ever restless, in the spring of 1905 he decided to try his hand at something new once again.

Five years had passed since sixteen-year-old, six-foot-tall Oscar Micheaux left Metropolis, Illinois, later to become the earthly home of the comic book character Superman. Young Micheaux was bored out of his gourd in his humdrum hometown. About the only thing that thrilled him was selling produce from his family's farm in the town's open-air market. Possessed with the gift of gab, he was a natural-born salesman.

OPPOSITE
Oscar Micheaux (c. 1913), by an unidentified photographer. Some pronounce his last name "Mee·show"; others say, "Mi·shaw." The surname he was born with was Michaux. He added an "e" while living in Chicago, where he also gave himself the middle name "Devereaux."

When Micheaux left Metropolis, he headed north, for Chicago. Now, in 1905, he headed west, to South Dakota, intent on being a homesteader. "I am here to make good, or die trying," he told a man over dinner, shortly after he bought his first 160 acres in Gregory County.

This black homesteader in overwhelmingly white South Dakota worked hard building a sod house, raising outbuildings, breaking up the earth, sowing and reaping, and getting his corn, flax, and other grain to market. He did not, however, make good. By the summer of 1912, his dream was a bust. First came blizzards, then came drought.

Crop failure wasn't the only thing that had Micheaux down in the dumps. Earlier, he had ended a budding romance with a Scottish woman, certain that if they kept on—if they married—life would be more difficult than it already was. He wound up marrying a black woman he had met in Chicago, Orlean McCracken—only she turned out to be a viper. So there he was in

the summer of 1912, not only broke but also brokenhearted.

Books were a big comfort. As this voracious reader lost himself in Jack London's *Martin Eden*, James Weldon Johnson's *Autobiography of an Ex-Colored Man*, and other stories, an idea took root. *Eureka!* It was as if he had struck gold!

During the fall of 1912, Oscar Micheaux wrote at a fever pitch, knocking out about two hundred pages by Christmas. He turned his life into a novel—homesteading, forbidden love, awful wife, and all. He hired one associate to edit his manuscript and another to type it up. He mailed the novel off to publishers. Then he waited.

When the rejections piled up, Micheaux didn't throw a pity party. Instead, he bucked up and decided to self-publish. And he was not about to let the fact that he was broke stand in his way. He suited up and blazed around South Dakota drumming up subscribers. In a matter of weeks he had presold fifteen hundred copies of his book

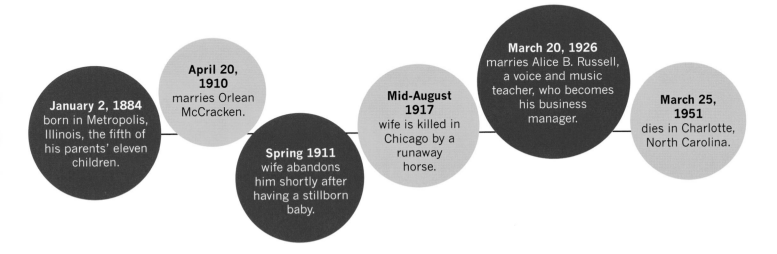

January 2, 1884 born in Metropolis, Illinois, the fifth of his parents' eleven children.

April 20, 1910 marries Orlean McCracken.

Spring 1911 wife abandons him shortly after having a stillborn baby.

Mid-August 1917 wife is killed in Chicago by a runaway horse.

March 20, 1926 marries Alice B. Russell, a voice and music teacher, who becomes his business manager.

March 25, 1951 dies in Charlotte, North Carolina.

at \$1.50 a pop. *The Conquest: The Story of a Negro Pioneer* was published on May 1, 1913.

Through mail-order and door-to-door sales (and with sales agents doing the same) Micheaux sold the heck out of *The Conquest* north, east, south, and west. His days as a Pullman porter definitely came in handy; while working as a servant in luxury railroad cars, he had been to scores of cities east and west of the Mississippi. Oscar Micheaux knew his way around.

While on the road selling *The Conquest*, this self-starter was fast at work on his next novel, *The Forged Note: A Romance of the Darker Races* (1915), which he also self-published. If that were not enough, while promoting *The Forged Note*, he worked on a revised edition of *The Conquest*, retitled *The Homesteader* (1917). As Micheaux watched *The Homesteader* outsell *The Conquest* ... *Eureka!* again. He decided to turn his novel into a picture show or photoplay, as movies were called.

In under a year Micheaux, long a lover of plays and movies, scripted his film, assembled a camera crew and a cast, scouted locations, directed the film, and publicized it. He had also wrangled friends and strangers into investing in his film, people as different as a German auctioneer in Sioux City and a black veterinarian working in a meatpacking plant in South Sioux City. There was also distribution: getting the film to screens. In those Jim Crow days, that usually meant black-only theaters and other black-only venues, some owned by blacks and some not.

When Micheaux got through wearing all those hats, he had made history. He was not the first black filmmaker, but he was the first to produce

An ad for Micheaux's film *The Homesteader* from the April 12, 1919, issue of the *Kansas City Sun*.

a full-length movie (a "super-production") versus a short (a film with a running time of forty minutes or less).

Micheaux's history-making film premiered at an armory in Chicago on February 20, 1919. Like other movies at the time, *The Homesteader*, which was about three hours long, was a silent film.

"The super-production, 'The Homesteader,' by Oscar Micheaux, negro author and producer, which opened at the Temple theater for a week's engagement last Sunday, has been meeting with great public appreciation." So said the *New Orleans Item* in June 1919. Later that summer, the *Washington Bee*, a black-owned weekly in the nation's capital, called *The Homesteader* "one of the most remarkable photoplays that has ever been exhibited in this city."

Micheaux was not a one-hit wonder. Fast and furious, from Chicago, New York, and elsewhere, he produced sometimes two or three films a year, giving people thrills and chills, making them laugh and cry. He also made them think: about race relations, the value of education, crime and punishment, the price of vice, the virtue of being true to oneself, and more.

The Dungeon (1922), *A Son of Satan* (1925), and *The Spider's Web* (1927) are some of Micheaux's early films. There was also *Body and Soul* (1925), about twin brothers—one saintly, one sinister—in which the already famous stage actor and singer Paul Robeson made his screen debut. Several years later Micheaux returned to his favorite subject (himself) with the first full-length talkie by a black filmmaker: *The Exile* (1931), the story of a homesteader in South Dakota.

Not every review was a rave. Not every flick was a hit. Still, many people applauded Micheaux for producing entertainment that did not limit black characters to buffoons and brutes, nitwits and ninnies, as Hollywood typically did. Micheaux's films reflected the diversity within his community. He peopled them with gangsters, gold miners, doctors,

IN HIS TIME

D. W. Griffith's silent film *The Birth of a Nation*, with its warped take on the Civil War–Reconstruction era, premiered under its original title *The Clansman* on February 8, 1915, and was released as *The Birth of a Nation* a few weeks later. This first full-length movie and a box-office smash caused a furor because it demonized black people and white abolitionists but glorified the Ku Klux Klan. The film sparked white-on-black individual and mob violence in Boston, New York, and other cities. *The Birth of a Nation* was the first film shown at the White House, an event that itself became controversial. After President Woodrow Wilson watched it, he congratulated Griffith on "a splendid production."

With the stock market crash of October 1929, came the Great Depression, which didn't end until World War II.

With the advent of talkies in the late 1920s, the movie business boomed. It boomed even more with the advent of Technicolor in the 1930s. MGM, Paramount, and 20th Century Fox were among the handful of studios that dominated in Hollywood during its "Golden Age" (the late 1920s through the early 1960s), a time of experimentation and adventures in a range of genres, from horror and gangster films to comedies and star-studded musicals. *The Wizard of Oz*, *It's a Wonderful Life*, and *King Kong* are among the classics from the Golden Age.

OPPOSITE A poster for Oscar Micheaux's first talkie. As in other films he produced, the "white" woman in *The Exile* turns out to be a light-skinned black woman.

Other Silver Screen Pioneers

Actor, reporter, and press agent **William D. Foster** (1884–1940) became a filmmaker in 1910 when he launched the Foster Photoplay Company in Chicago. When the company folded a few years later, Foster had produced a handful of comedic shorts: *The Fall Guy*; *The Butler*; *The Grafter and the Maid*; and his most successful film, *The Railroad Porter* (1912).

In 1916, actor **Noble Johnson** (1881–1978) cofounded the Lincoln Motion Picture Company, an outfit that was based in Los Angeles, California, for most of its life. When it ceased operations in 1923, Lincoln had produced several silents. The first was *The Realization of a Negro's Ambition* (1916), a twenty-minute short about a young civil engineer who makes a fortune in the oil business.

lawyers, teachers, detectives, and millionaires. As he stated in a press release, "I have always tried to make my photoplays present the truth, to lay before the race a cross section of its own life—to view the colored heart from close range."

In his truth telling, Oscar Micheaux used "film methods that were as idiosyncratic and modern-minded as anything being tried in Hollywood at that time," observed biographer Patrick McGilligan. These techniques included multiple points of view, flashbacks, intercutting, and crosscutting.

To be sure, Micheaux's films were not as polished as those Hollywood produced, but unlike Hollywood directors, Micheaux did not have budgets of $100,000, $200,000, $300,000 and up. The man from Metropolis made his magic with about $15,000 on average. It takes a kind of genius to do that. A superman of sorts.

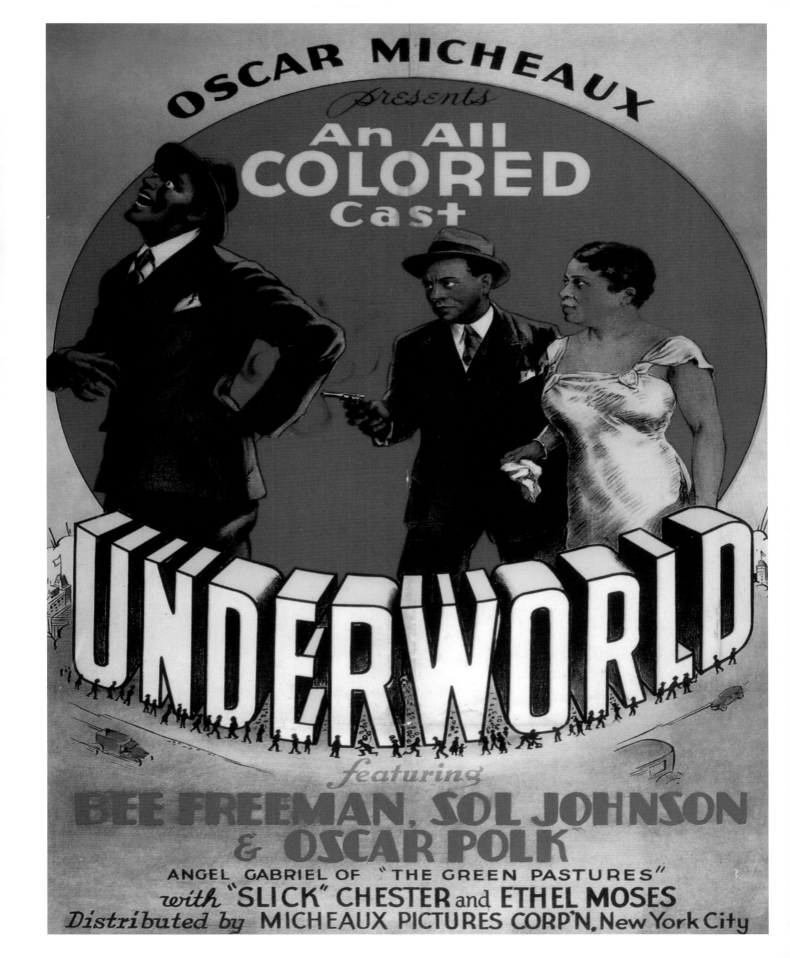

CARTOONIST

Jackie Ormes

1911–1985

In the 1920s, many teenagers had to work after school and on weekends or even drop out of school altogether to help their families out. Not Jackie. As a girl growing up in Monongahela, Pennsylvania, she was free to focus on her schoolwork and other pursuits. Her family wasn't rich, but comfortable enough that the kids didn't have to work.

At Monongahela High, where Jackie and her older sister, Delores, were among the few people of color, schoolwork included algebra, geometry, ancient history, modern history, French, and Latin. Jackie also had the freedom to take on extracurricular activities, such as being in the French Club. And this girl had plenty of time for her passion—art.

OPPOSITE Jackie Ormes in the area of her apartment that served as her studio (1946), by an unidentified photographer. Along with cartooning, Ormes did illustrations for ads, produced fashion shows, and trained models.

Baby Jackie flanked by her father, William Winfield Jackson, owner of a print shop and an outdoor picture show, and her mother, Mary Brown Jackson, a homemaker. The little girl standing is Jackie's sister, Delores. This photo was taken about 1912 by an unidentified photographer.

Her drawing talent landed her a spot on the high school yearbook, *The Flame*. Senior year she served as its arts editor. By then she had her eye on journalism. Before she even graduated from high school, Jackie wrote to Robert Vann, publisher of the *Pittsburgh Courier*, a leading black-owned newspaper. Her letter is long gone, so we don't exactly how this spunky young woman pitched herself. Whatever she said worked. Vann gave her a shot.

Jackie's first assignment—reporting on a prizefight—was not for the fainthearted. She didn't wimp out and in fact loved every minute of the bout. And the *Courier* was clearly pleased with her work. After graduating from high school in 1930, Jackie moved to Pittsburgh to work for the newspaper as an assistant proofreader and occasional reporter.

As it turned out, drawing trumped journalism. After several years at the *Courier*, Jackie Ormes talked Vann into letting her contribute to the paper's funny pages.

Ormes's *Torchy Brown in "Dixie to Harlem,"* a four-frame comic strip, had its debut in the *Courier* on May 1, 1937. It's the saga of a teenage girl who finds life on a farm in Mississippi a total yawn—and she's nervy enough to do something about it.

After selling some farm animals for train fare, Torchy heads to New York City, where she has a rollicking time. In one strip she's at a prizefight, rooting for Joe "the Brown Bomber" Louis, shouting, "Yoo-hoo CHES! Atta Joe—Poke 'im—He's down—Whee!" *Torchy Brown in "Dixie to Harlem"* had only a twelve-month run, but Jackie Ormes was not down for the count.

Ormes made a comeback in March 1945 in another major black-owned weekly, the *Chicago Defender*. This time her creation, *Candy*, a single-panel gag cartoon, starred a beautiful, smart housemaid full of wisecracks about her employer, Mrs. Goldrocks (who is never seen). Clever Candy had an even

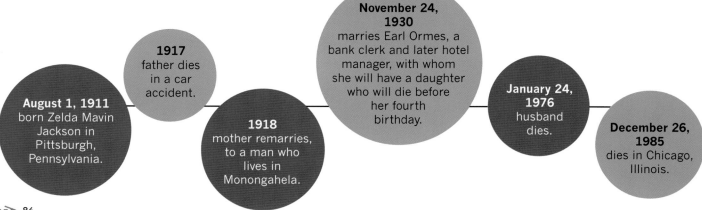

August 1, 1911
born Zelda Mavin Jackson in Pittsburgh, Pennsylvania.

1917
father dies in a car accident.

1918
mother remarries, to a man who lives in Monongahela.

November 24, 1930
marries Earl Ormes, a bank clerk and later hotel manager, with whom she will have a daughter who will die before her fourth birthday.

January 24, 1976
husband dies.

December 26, 1985
dies in Chicago, Illinois.

"Funny Side Up" was a two-page collection of caricatures printed in Monongahela High's 1930 yearbook, *The Flame*. During her professional career, Jackie Ormes sometimes used her given name Zelda, as she did in this artwork.

In 1935, educator and activist Mary McLeod Bethune founded the National Council of Negro Women (NCNW), an umbrella organization of dozens of black women's organizations devoted to social, political, and economic justice.

In June 1938, DC Comics introduced the first superhero, Superman, in *Action Comics #1*. In January 1939 the man of steel had his own newspaper comic strip and, starting in the summer of 1939, his own comic book series. It was also in 1939 that DC Comics brought out the caped crusader originally named "The Bat-Man." In 1941, the company introduced the first major female superhero, "Wonder Woman." *Brenda Starr, Reporter* (1940) and *Peanuts* (1950) were among the popular comic strips during the Golden Age of Comics (late 1930s–early 1950s).

A polio outbreak in the 1940s and early 1950s crippled or killed about thirty thousand people in the United States. Many of the victims were children. Jonas Salk developed a vaccine in 1955.

Torchy meets the famous tap dancer Bill "Bojangles" Robinson in this *Dixie to Harlem* strip that ran in the *Pittsburgh Courier* on January 22, 1938.

shorter run than Torchy (March 24, 1945–July 21, 1945), but again, it wasn't over for Ormes. On September 1, 1945, she was back in the pages of the *Pittsburgh Courier* with another single-panel cartoon.

It was an idea Ormes had been toying with for a while: a cartoon that didn't star a teenage girl or a woman but rather a little girl: five-year-old Patty-Jo. Quick with the lip, strong-willed, and sassy, Patty-Jo constantly gives her big sister, Ginger, grief and does zany things like drop tadpoles into a glass of lemonade. Though Patty-Jo is a rough-and-tumble kid, whether in an ice cream parlor, at the cinema, or walking down the street, she is always smartly dressed.

Along with spunk, Jackie Ormes gave Patty-Jo a big heart. The little girl wishes for world peace. She empties her piggy bank so she can join the NAACP. She also supports the March of Dimes, the organization President Franklin Roosevelt started in 1938 in his war on polio, a disease he contracted in 1921 at the age of thirty-nine.

Patty-Jo 'n' Ginger ran for eleven years in the *Courier*. Counting the newspaper's editions in New York, Philadelphia, Washington, D.C., and ten other cities, at one point the *Pittsburgh Courier* was letting roughly one million subscribers and their families and friends know exactly what was on the mind and in the imagination of Jackie Ormes, who followed her childhood passion and, in doing so, became the first black woman in the United States to have a career as a cartoonist.

"What'cha mean it's no game for girls? We got feet too, ain't we?"

From the October 15, 1949, issue of the *Pittsburgh Courier*. The character of Patty-Jo became so popular that there was even a Patty-Jo doll. During *Patty-Jo 'n' Gingers's* run, Ormes revisited her character Torchy Brown, still up for adventures along with crusading for justice. And romance. The second Torchy strip, which ran in the *Pittsburgh Courier* from 1950 to 1954 was first titled *Torchy Brown Heartbeats*, then *Torchy in Heartbeats*.

ECONOMIST
& ATTORNEY

Sadie Tanner Mossell Alexander

1898–1989

"Not one woman . . . spoke to me in class. . . or on the walks to College Hall or the Library. Can you imagine looking for classrooms and asking persons the way, only to find the same unresponsive person you asked for directions seated in the classroom in which you entered late because you could not find your way?"

That's what Sadie had to deal with in 1915 when she entered Philadelphia's University of Pennsylvania, which had very few black students. As she later pointed out, the treatment she received "made a student either a dropout or [a] survivor so strong that she could not be overcome, regardless of the indignities."

OPPOSITE *Sadie T. M. Alexander* (June 15, 1921), photograph by Gilbert & Bacon. When she earned her PhD in 1921, fewer than 15 percent of Americans between the ages of seventeen and twenty attended college.

Drop out? Not Sadie, a graduate of the prestigious M Street High School in Washington, D.C., and a young woman with many high achievers in her family tree.

Sadie did not drop out of college when white students ignored her, nor when a professor chased her and another woman from his class, refusing to teach women, nor when she faced other hostilities. What's more, in pursuit of a bachelor's degree in education, Sadie did not merely stick it out—she excelled. In 1918 she graduated with honors. And she did it in three years instead of the usual four.

Next challenge: a master's degree in the difficult field of economics. Done, in 1919!

Next challenge: a PhD in economics. Done, in 1921—and the first black American to earn a doctorate in that field!

Next challenge: find a job.

Not so easily done.

"I couldn't get work anywhere," she said in a 1976 interview. "In fact, the situation was such in Philadelphia that I could not even have taught high school after I had gotten all this training because they didn't employ any colored teachers."

After several Philadelphia white-owned insurance firms refused to hire this brilliant woman, Sadie happily accepted

Sadie Tanner Mossell Alexander (c. 1905), by an unidentified photographer. She was about seven years old.

January 2, 1898 born in Philadelphia, Pennsylvania, the youngest of her parents' three children.

c. January 1899 father leaves the family, moving to Cardiff, Wales.

November 29, 1923 marries Raymond Pace Alexander, with whom she will have two daughters.

November 24, 1974 husband dies.

November 1, 1989 dies in Philadelphia, Pennsylvania.

a job in Durham, North Carolina. The position was as an assistant actuary at the black-owned North Carolina Mutual Life Insurance Company. There she analyzed the economic fallout of risks and uncertainties, the basis for setting insurance premiums. That lasted for about two years—until love brought her home.

His name was Raymond Pace Alexander, another University of Pennsylvania alum. In 1920, Raymond became the first black person to graduate from Penn's Wharton School of Finance and Commerce. After that, he earned a law degree from Harvard Law School. Now that he had passed the Pennsylvania bar and hung out his shingle, renting two rooms in an office building on Broad and Lombard Streets, the couple was ready to marry.

Done, in 1923!

After her wedding, Sadie did what most people expected a middle-class married woman to do: be a homemaker. But that was not a good fit for her. "I stayed home for one year and almost lost my mind." She needed another challenge.

In 1927, when the United States had fewer than four thousand women lawyers and only a handful of black women lawyers, Sadie Tanner Mossell Alexander became the first black woman to graduate from the University of Pennsylvania Law School. Typical: she graduated with honors.

After she was admitted to the Pennsylvania bar—a first for a black woman—her husband, who had paid her law school tuition, was eager for her to join his law firm, which by then occupied an entire floor of a building on Nineteenth and Chestnut Streets. When a partner balked at having a woman lawyer on the team, Raymond Alexander gave this black man a choice: accept it or leave. (The man stayed.)

Sadie Alexander, who specialized in family, estate, and property law, often worked with her husband on cases in his areas of expertise: criminal defense and civil rights. Together they drafted a bill to prohibit

Mossell Family, group portrait (c. 1875), by an unidentified photographer. Seated center: Sadie's father's parents, Aaron and Eliza Mossell. Around them are their children (left to right): Mary, Alvaretta, Charles, Aaron Albert (Sadie's father), and Nathan Francis. Sadie's father (1856–1946) was the first black person to graduate from the University of Pennsylvania Law School (1888). Her uncle Nathan was the first black person to graduate from the University of Pennsylvania School of Medicine (1882). He founded Philadelphia's Frederick Douglass Memorial Hospital and Training School in 1895. Illustrious members of the Tanner family include Sadie's grandfather, Benjamin Tucker Tanner, a bishop in the African Methodist Episcopal Church and a graduate of Avery College (1870) and Wilberforce University (1878); her uncle Henry, a world-renowned painter; and her aunt Halle, a graduate of the Women's Medical College in Philadelphia and founder of the Tuskegee Institute Training School of Nurses (now part of Tuskegee University) in Alabama.

In June 1941 President Franklin Roosevelt issued Executive Order 8802, prohibiting discriminatory employment practices in federal agencies, unions, and companies engaged in national defense work for the government.

President Harry Truman issued Executive Order 9981 on July 26, 1948, mandating equal opportunity and treatment of people in the armed forces regardless of race, color, religion, or national origin.

On May 17, 1954, the U.S. Supreme Court declared segregated public schools unconstitutional when it ruled in the case *Brown v. Board of Education*.

The Montgomery Bus Boycott, sparked by Rosa Parks's act of civil disobedience and led by Martin Luther King Jr., began on December 1, 1955. It ended thirteen months later, after the U.S. Supreme Court upheld a lower court's ruling that segregated seating on public buses was unconstitutional.

racial discrimination in Pennsylvania's restaurants, theaters, and hotels. Their work culminated in Pennsylvania's 1935 Equal Rights Law.

The couple's teamwork lasted until 1959, when Raymond Alexander closed his practice, having become another first: the first black person appointed a judge on Philadelphia's Court of Common Pleas, Pennsylvania's highest trial court. By then, among other things, Sadie Alexander had become the first black woman to serve as Philadelphia's assistant solicitor (1927–31 and 1936–40). What's more, in 1946 President Harry Truman had appointed her to his Committee on Civil Rights. She was one of two blacks and two women on this commission, which included labor leader John Carey and Morris Ernst, cofounder of the American Civil Liberties Union. The fifteen-member body was tasked with investigating the state of civil rights in America. Its nearly two-hundred-page groundbreaking report, *To Secure These Rights* (October 1947), documented racial injustices and disparities and urged action: from the enactment of anti-lynching laws to ending segregation in public schools.

And Sadie was not done!

After her husband closed his law practice, she opened her own, and she didn't shutter it until 1976, when she was seventy-eight. A few years later, when asked what advice she had for young people, Dr. Sadie Tanner Mossell Alexander replied, "Don't let anything stop you. There will be times when you'll be disappointed, but you can't stop. Make yourself the best that you can make out of what you are. The very best."

Fewer than a thousand people in the United States earned doctorates in 1921. Along with Sadie Tanner Mossell Alexander, two other black women earned PhDs that year.

Georgiana Rose Simpson (1866–1944) graduated on June 14, 1921, from the University of Chicago with a PhD in German. This native of Washington was in her fifties when she finished graduate school, because while earning her bachelor's degree at the University of Chicago, she often had to postpone classes until summer or take correspondence courses to avoid masses of hostile white students. After she received her PhD, Simpson taught German and French at Washington's Paul Dunbar High School (formerly the M Street High School), where she had taught in the past. In 1931, she became a professor of German at the city's Howard University.

Rae Pace, Mary Elizabeth, Sadie and Raymond Alexander, in Front of Their Christmas Tree (c. 1943), photograph by G. Marshall Wilson. When this photograph was taken, the Alexander family lived at 1708 West Jefferson Street in Philadelphia. They also had a country house, "Skywater," near Coatesville, Pennsylvania.

Washingtonian **Eva Beatrice Dykes** (1893–1986) graduated from Radcliffe College with a PhD in English on June 22, 1921. Radcliffe (now part of Harvard University) is where Dykes had earned her master's degree and a second bachelor's degree (magna cum laude), after having earned a bachelor's degree (summa cum laude) from Howard University. After she earned her PhD, with her expertise in English, German, Greek, and Latin, Dykes also taught at Paul Laurence Dunbar High School, as well as at several colleges, including Howard University and Oakwood College (now University) in Huntsville, Alabama.

ARCHITECT

Paul R. Williams

1894–1980

"Who ever heard of a Negro being an architect?" scoffed a teacher at Polytechnic High in Los Angeles, California. The man stared at Paul "with as much astonishment as he would have displayed had I proposed a rocket flight to Mars." If the teen or anyone else had named black architects they *had* heard of—MIT graduate Robert R. Taylor, for example— the teacher might have laughed in their faces.

"You have ability," the teacher told Paul, and then advised him to use it in another pursuit. The man believed that to make it as an architect, one needed white clients. That wouldn't, couldn't happen to Paul, he was sure. "Don't butt your head futilely against the stone wall of race prejudice."

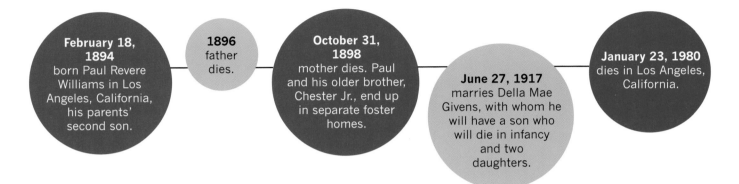

February 18, 1894
born Paul Revere Williams in Los Angeles, California, his parents' second son.

1896 father dies.

October 31, 1898
mother dies. Paul and his older brother, Chester Jr., end up in separate foster homes.

June 27, 1917
marries Della Mae Givens, with whom he will have a son who will die in infancy and two daughters.

January 23, 1980
dies in Los Angeles, California.

It hurt to have his dream trashed like that. Paul, who had loved to draw since he was a little boy, had been dreaming of being an architect for years.

Don't butt your head futilely against the stone wall of race prejudice.

Paul thought long and hard about his teacher's advice. In the end, he reasoned that if he let the fact that he was black "checkmate my will to do, now, I will inevitably form the habit of being defeated." He decided to be hardheaded.

After graduating from Polytechnic High in 1912, Paul began teaching himself everything he could about architecture, and in three years he was a certified building contractor. He also took advantage of the L.A. Architectural Club. As a member, he could attend classes and enter competitions sponsored by the Society of Beaux-Arts Architects, another club. Added to that, he studied at the University of Southern California for three years, leaving before he could graduate because he needed to work.

While he worked, he did a lot of what he called "art school 'hopping'": taking courses nights and weekends at several art schools, where different teachers taught different techniques.

In his skill-building mission, Williams entered several competitions, winning some. The Hollow Tile House Competition in 1919 was one. The challenge he and twenty-three other contenders accepted was to design a one-story house that could be built for no more than $5,000 and using hollow tiles (a type of brick). The judges praised Williams for avoiding "useless ornaments or expensive fads" in awarding him the first-place prize of $300.

While studying architecture and entering competitions, Paul R. Williams also worked at several white-owned architectural firms that specialized in different things—one in landscape architecture, another in luxury homes, another in commercial buildings. And it all added up. Having become astute in physics and architectural engineering,

HOUSE No. 150

Designed by Paul R. Williams, Los Angeles, Calif.

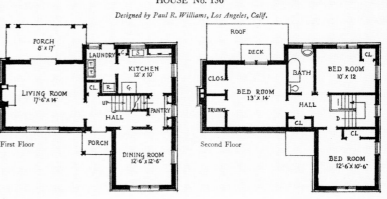

having become a master with slide rules, compasses, angle gauges, and other tools, nine years after he graduated from high school, in June 1921, Williams was a licensed architect. In 1922 he took what he called "the great step." He opened a practice of his own.

When Paul R. Williams and Associates opened in L.A.'s Stock Exchange Building, it was a one-man band. His early commissions included a home on South Serrano Avenue for Louis M. Blodgett, a black contractor and, in collaboration with white architect Norman F. Marsh, the Second Baptist Church, a historically black church. Understanding that to succeed in life one often must stoop to conquer, Williams often took on small projects that larger firms turned down.

Along the way, Williams had his share of disappointments. Some potential commissions became dust in the wind when a white person, perhaps having seen some of his work, came to his office and only then discovered that he was black. "I could see many of them 'freeze,'" he told readers of the *American Magazine* in 1937. In this same article, Williams shared one of the secrets of his success. No matter the size of a job, he gave it his all. "I labored over the plans for a $15,000 residence as diligently as I do today over the plans for a huge mansion." Mansion?

Yes. Williams had quite a few high-profile projects under his belt by then.

One of Williams's first commissions for a mansion was for Cordhaven: E. L. Cord's 32,000-square-foot home on his eighteen-acre estate in Beverly Hills. This white industrialist had telephoned Williams out of the blue one day and asked—more like demanded—that Williams meet with him

"House No. 150," from the American Face Brick Association's sixth edition of *The Home of Beauty: Designs for a Small Brick House* (1925). Williams's design for this brick cottage was one of four hundred entries in a competition sponsored by the journal *Architectural Forum*. Although Williams's design wasn't the winner, it won a place in *The Home of Beauty*.

Cordhaven (c. 1939), by an unidentified photographer. This Southern Colonial–style redbrick mansion had sixteen bedrooms, twenty-two bathrooms, two huge kitchens, and three dining rooms, as well as a ballroom, a billiard room, and other leisure spaces. The estate also had a pool house and stables.

straightaway at the building site. Williams obliged, sizing Cord up as a man who "worshipped prompt action." At the end of the meeting, Cord asked Williams when he could deliver preliminary drawings.

"By four o'clock tomorrow afternoon," Williams replied.

"Why, that's impossible!" Cord responded. "Every other architect has asked for two or three weeks!" Taking the measure of this man, he then said, "Go ahead."

Williams met the deadline and clinched the deal, never telling Cord that he had "worked for twenty-two hours, without sleeping or eating," as he later wrote.

Cord's two-million-dollar showplace, completed during the Great Depression, in 1933, really put Paul R. Williams on the map. He designed many more luxury homes in Beverly Hills, as well as in Bel Air and other posh places in California, for a galaxy of white movie stars—so many

Wallace A. Rayfield (1873–1941), born in Macon, Georgia, studied architecture at two New York schools: Brooklyn's Pratt Polytechnic Institute and Manhattan's Columbia University, where he earned his bachelor's degree in architecture (1899). Rayfield taught architectural courses at Alabama's Tuskegee Institute (now University), where architect Robert Taylor was director of industries. While still working at Tuskegee, Rayfield opened his own office in 1907, then relocated to Birmingham in 1908. Of the four hundred or more homes, schools, stores, churches, and other edifices Rayfield designed, one of the best known is the Sixteenth Street Baptist Church, where several people were injured and four girls killed when, shortly before the morning worship service on Sunday, September 15, 1963 (Youth Day), members of the Ku Klux Klan bombed it.

Born in Harlem, New York, to a father from Trinidad and a mother from Venezuela, **Norma Merrick Sklarek** (1926–2012) was the first black woman in the United States to become a licensed architect. She received her license in 1954, four years after earning her bachelor's degree from Columbia University School of Architecture. For twenty years Sklarek worked at Gruen Associates, a prominent L.A.-based firm, where she became its first black director of architecture in 1966. In 1985, with two white women, she founded a firm of her own: Siegal-Sklarek-Diamond. Sklarek's best-known designs include the city hall of San Bernardino, California, and the U.S. embassy in Tokyo, Japan.

Clarence "Cap" Wigington (1883–1967), who grew up in Omaha, Nebraska, became the principal designer for the office of municipal architecture in Saint Paul, Minnesota (1915–49). The Highland Park Water Tower (1928), the Hamline and Minnehaha playground buildings (1938 and 1940), the Harriet Island Pavilion (1941, now the Clarence W. Wigington Pavilion), and several ice palaces for the Saint Paul Winter Carnival are among the most beloved creations of this man who never got a degree in architecture. Wigington honed his skills by working as a draftsman for six years after graduating high school. His boss/mentor was a white architect in Omaha, the renowned Thomas R. Kimball.

After World War II, the United States and the Soviet Union, once allies, engaged in a "Cold War": an economic, ideological, and military rivalry, with the United States promoting a capitalist economy and a democratic government and the Soviet Union promoting a communist economy and government. The Cold War wouldn't end until 1991.

The Korean War began on June 25, 1950, with the United States backing South Korea and the Soviet Union backing North Korea. It ended on July 27, 1953.

A CIA-engineered attempt to overthrow Fidel Castro's communist rule in Cuba failed in April 1961 after U.S.-backed bombers missed their targets on the island and an invasion force of 1,400 Cuban exiles came under fire when they landed at its Bay of Pigs.

In May 1961, President John F. Kennedy authorized the deployment of 500 Special Forces troops and military advisers to aid South Vietnam in its war against the Soviet Union–backed North Vietnam. Between the time of this increased American presence in Vietnam and the U.S. agreement to a cease-fire in early 1973, some 2.7 million Americans served in Vietnam, over 300,000 were wounded, and approximately 58,000 died. The war ended with South Vietnam's surrender on April 30, 1975.

Fear of a nuclear war gripped the world for thirteen days in October 1962 when the United States and the Soviet Union faced off over nuclear missiles in Cuba, ninety miles off the coast of Florida. The Cuban Missile Crisis ended when the Soviet Union's leader, Nikita Khrushchev, agreed to remove his missiles from Cuba and the U.S. president, John F. Kennedy, pledged that his country would never invade or again support an invasion of Cuba. The world later learned that President Kennedy had also promised to remove U.S. missiles recently installed in Turkey, on the border it shared with the Soviet Union.

that he became known as the "Architect to the Stars." The luminaries included Lon Chaney, Barbara Stanwyck, Johnny Weissmuller, Frank Sinatra, and Lucille Ball. Tap dancer Bill "Bojangles" Robinson was among his black celebrity clients.

Williams also worked on commercial buildings. The more than twenty he designed or codesigned in Los Angeles alone include the Beverly Hills Hotel, the Los Angeles County Courthouse, Saks Fifth Ave, the 28th Street YMCA, and the Theme Building at Los Angeles International Airport (LAX).

LAX's Theme Building opened in 1962, the same year that Saint Jude's Children's Research Hospital opened in Memphis, Tennessee. Williams donated his design for Saint Jude's, founded by his friend Danny Thomas, a Lebanese American actor and TV producer. Saint Jude's, which pledged to not discriminate against any child because of race, became a leading research and treatment hospital for children with cancer and other serious diseases.

It was also in 1962 that Williams donated the design for the First African Methodist Episcopal Church's new sanctuary on 25th and LaSalle Streets. By then Paul R. Williams and Associates, located on Wilshire Boulevard, employed about two dozen people.

When Williams retired in the 1970s, he had worked on more than three thousand projects in the States and abroad. If that teacher from Polytechnic High was still alive, he must have been awestruck by how his student's hardheadedness had paid off.

Paul R. Williams (1965), by Julius Shulman. When this photograph was taken of Williams standing in front of LAX's Theme Building, which he codesigned, the architect had, among other things, opened an office in Bogota, Colombia; been licensed to practice in New York, Tennessee, and Nevada; served as president of the Advisory Committee of the State of California's U.S. Commission on Civil Rights; and been appointed to the National Housing Commission by President Dwight Eisenhower. He had also been elected to the American Institute of Architects College of Fellows. Back in 1923, Williams had become the first black person elected to this prestigious professional architectural association.

MATHEMATICIAN

Katherine Coleman Goble Johnson

1918–

"I was born liking math," eighty-year-old Katherine Johnson told a reporter in 1998. "I counted the steps. I counted the plates that I washed. I counted everything."

Young Katherine did that counting in White Sulphur Springs, West Virginia, where she entered elementary school as a second grader at the age of four. Going through school in leaps and bounds, this math prodigy was poised to start high school at age ten in 1928. But there was a problem. Her hometown had no high school for blacks.

OPPOSITE Katherine Johnson, age seventeen, at West Virginia State College, by an unidentified photographer, 1936–37.

TOP *NACA High Speed Flight Station "Computer Room"* (1949), by an unidentified photographer. Left, beneath the Friden dustcover, is presumably a Friden mechanical calculator.

ABOVE Johnson on the job c. 1956, by an unknown photographer.

Katherine's parents solved the problem by making major sacrifices. During the school year, her father remained in White Sulphur Springs while her mother took her and her siblings to live in Institute, West Virginia, more than a hundred miles away. Institute, about eight miles from Charleston, was home to historically black West Virginia Collegiate Institute. And it had a high school.

Katherine thrived at that high school. On top of being a brainiac, she had the kind of personality that was a magnet for mentors. One was her geometry teacher, Angie Turner King. "A wonderful teacher—bright, caring, and very rigorous," Katherine later described King, who had earned her bachelor's degree, cum laude, in mathematics and chemistry from the Institute (and later earned a PhD in mathematics and chemistry from the University of Pittsburgh). Another of Katherine's mentors was Principal Sherman H. Guss. He sparked this bright girl's interest in astronomy by identifying stars during evening walks.

By the time fifteen-year-old Katherine was ready for college in 1933, the Institute had become West Virginia State College. There her mentors included the head of the Romance languages department, Professor John F. Matthews, who spoke seven languages. Probably no professor had as great an impact on Katherine as did Dr. William Waldron Schiefflin Claytor, the third black American to earn a PhD in mathematics (1933). Spying in Katherine a particular ability, Dr. Claytor one day told her, "You'd make a good research mathematician and I'm going to see that you're prepared." When Katherine asked what research mathematicians do, Dr. Claytor replied, "You'll find out." It was many years before she did.

August 26, 1918
born Katherine Coleman in White Sulphur Springs, West Virginia, the youngest of her parents' four children.

December 5, 1939
marries James Francis Goble, a schoolteacher, with whom she will have three daughters.

December 20, 1956
husband dies.

August 22, 1959
marries James A. Johnson, a captain in the Army Reserves and war veteran.

After she graduated summa cum laude from college in 1937 at age eighteen, with a degree in mathematics and French, Katherine didn't seek work as a research mathematician. Instead, she taught mathematics and sometimes French at several schools in West Virginia, then in Virginia. Not until the early 1950s did Katherine Johnson seize an opportunity to fulfill Dr. Claytor's prediction.

While visiting in-laws in Newport News, Virginia, in 1952, Johnson learned that the National Advisory Committee for Aeronautics (NACA) in nearby Hampton, Virginia, was hiring women with math skills. By the time she got her application in, all the slots had been filled.

Disappointed? Yes.

Defeated? No.

She applied again the following year. This time she landed a job as a research mathematician at NACA, which had started experimenting with supersonic flight in the late 1940s. For all the calculations required for this work, NACA didn't have high-speed electronic computers to rely on. As Johnson later explained, this was at a time when "computers wore skirts." Like other women crunching numbers for NACA engineers, Johnson did it the old-fashioned way: with slide rules and mechanical calculators.

Then came the Space Age. Katherine Johnson's duties changed.

On October 4, 1957, the Soviet Union launched Sputnik 1, the first artificial satellite. The United States was not going to sit on the sidelines while the Soviet Union, its archenemy, explored outer space. A year after Sputnik, NACA became NASA (the National Aeronautics and Space Administration). Now the United States was in the business of exploring space, too.

IN HER TIME

On August 28, 1963, about a quarter million people participated in the March on Washington for Jobs and Freedom, where Dr. Martin Luther King Jr. delivered his speech, "I Have a Dream."

Between late 1963 and the spring of 1968, President Lyndon Johnson succeeded in getting about two dozen laws passed for programs and initiatives to improve the lives of everyday Americans. These "Great Society" programs included Medicare, health care for senior citizens. There was also Head Start, a summer-school program for children from low-income families that evolved into an early-childhood program for this population, offering educational, health, and other services. Another Great Society initiative was the expansion and renovation of public housing.

President Johnson signed three major civil rights laws in the 1960s: the Civil Rights Act of 1964, which banned discrimination in public places and facilities; the 1965 Voting Rights Act, which outlawed literacy tests, poll taxes, and other methods local and state governments had instituted to suppress the black vote; and the Civil Rights Act of 1968, aimed at ending discrimination in housing, from sale and rental to financing.

The 1960s was a decade of tumult on many fronts. Along with boycotts, sit-ins, and marches for black people's civil rights, there were rallies and marches against U.S. involvement in the Vietnam War and for women's rights.

Several historic American figures were assassinated during the 1960s. Among them were Medgar Evers and President John F. Kennedy in 1963; Malcolm X in 1965; Martin Luther King Jr. and Robert F. Kennedy in 1968; and Black Panther Fred Hampton in 1969.

Sex discrimination in education became illegal on June 23, 1972, when the Education Amendments of 1972 went into effect.

Another Math Whiz

Chicago, Illinois, native **J. Ernest Wilkins Jr.** (1923–2011) began his freshman year at the University of Chicago in the fall of 1936, at the age of thirteen. After earning his bachelor's and master's degrees in mechanical engineering, he received a PhD in mathematics at nineteen. Wilkins became a leading mathematician and nuclear engineer. Some of the problem-solving he did was for a 1940s top-secret research project, the Manhattan Project, which produced the first atomic bomb.

"Everything was so new—the whole idea of going into space was new and daring," said Johnson years later. "There were no textbooks, so we had to write them." Johnson and other "human computers" also had to contend with sexism in those early years. For example, these women were not allowed to attend briefings and were not permitted to have their names on their research. Still, they soldiered on. Johnson, who was promoted to aerospace technologist in 1958, coauthored twenty-eight research reports. One of them was "The Determination of Azimuth Angle at Burnout for Placing a Satellite over a Selected Earth Position." This 1960 paper paved the way for getting spacecraft into and back from outer space.

During a long and stellar career at NASA, Johnson's work included charting the course for Alan Shepard's suborbital flight aboard *Freedom 7* on May 5, 1961, the first U.S. voyage into space. When an electronic computer was used to calculate the trajectory for John Glenn's historic orbital flight, to occur on February 20, 1962, Katherine Johnson still had a key role to play. John Glenn wasn't keen on putting his mission—and his life—in the hands of a machine. He requested that Johnson verify the computer's calculations. A few years later came an even greater challenge for Johnson: calculating the paths that *Apollo 11* would take to and from the moon.

On July 20, 1969, when Neil Armstrong became the first person in the world to set foot on the lunar surface—making his "one small step," which represented "one giant leap for mankind"—Johnson was ecstatic! But not until four days later, when mission commander Armstrong and his crewmates, Michael Collins and Edwin "Buzz" Aldrin, had a successful splashdown in the Pacific Ocean, about eight hundred miles southwest of Hawaii, did this human computer rest easy. Only then did Katherine Johnson know that she had gotten all the numbers right.

On November 24, 2015, Barack Obama bestowed upon this STEM pioneer the Presidential Medal of Freedom, the nation's highest civilian honor.

ABOVE Johnson (*far right*) with colleagues in 1970 at NASA Langley Research Center, by an unidentified photographer.

OPPOSITE *Launch of Apollo 11* (July 16, 1969) at the Kennedy Space Center in Cape Canaveral, Florida, by an unidentified photographer.

When Katherine Johnson and her colleagues at NASA celebrated the *Apollo 11* mission in 1969, much had changed since young Broteer Furro / Venture Smith laid eyes on Newport, Rhode Island, two hundred thirty years earlier.

In 1969, slavery had been abolished for more than one hundred years through the Thirteenth Amendment (1865).

Women had gained the right to vote about fifty years earlier through the Nineteenth Amendment (1920).

Fifteen years before Neil Armstrong's moonwalk, government-sanctioned segregation had been dealt a death blow when the U.S. Supreme Court ruled that segregated public schooling was unconstitutional in its *Brown v. Board of Education* decision.

Racial prejudice and sexism were still intense, injustices still immense, but in this much-changed United States more doors of opportunities were opening for people of African descent. Just as Venture Smith, James Forten, Maggie Lena Walker, Oscar Micheaux, Charlie Wiggins, Katherine Johnson, and the other intrepid souls in this book had done, legions of blacks in America with grit and guts and goals were making giant strides while others were charting a course for success. In science and technology. In education. In the fine, performing, literary, and culinary arts. In finance. In business.

Willy T. Ribbs graduated from high school in 1975, intent on having a professional auto racing career—which he did, breaking the Indy 500 color barrier in 1991.

Neil deGrasse Tyson graduated from the Bronx High School of Science in 1976, then pursued a path that led to his becoming an astrophysicist.

Also in 1976, a young woman with a hard-luck childhood and an odd first name that begins with "O" was hosting a Baltimore-based TV show, *People Are Talking*. To be sure, she was aiming to rise in her industry but probably never expecting to become a media mogul and a billionaire.

And when Oprah Winfrey was hosting that Baltimore show, Mae C. Jemison was at Stanford University earning a bachelor's degree in chemical engineering. She would follow that up with a medical degree from Cornell and later aim even higher, becoming NASA's first black woman astronaut. Jemison journeyed into space aboard a ship named *Endeavour* on September 2, 1992, two days after future history-making ballerina Misty Copeland was born in Kansas City, Missouri.

This is a very small sampling of people who were shooting for the moon in this new America. In every state in the nation new odysseys were in the offing. As they are today.

Misty Copeland in *Le Corsaire* (2013), photographed by Rosalie O'Connor.
In June 2015, Copeland became the first black woman promoted to
principal dancer in the prestigious American Ballet Theatre. This
New York City–based company was founded in 1940.

GLOSSARY

abolitionist: someone who advocates for the immediate end of slavery.

American Civil Liberties Union (ACLU): a not-for-profit organization founded in 1920 and pledged to "defend and preserve the individual rights and liberties guaranteed to every person in this country by the Constitution and laws of the United States." The ACLU's founders included author and activist Helen Keller and social workers Jane Addams and Roger Baldwin.

antebellum: existing before the Civil War.

apprentice: a person who spends a period of time learning a trade from someone already highly skilled in that trade.

Confederacy, the: the states that seceded from the United States in the months leading up to and at the start of the Civil War.

dispatch: a message, usually sent quickly.

émigré: someone who leaves their native land to settle in another country, often for political reasons.

Fitzgerald, F. Scott (1896–1940): an American short story writer and novelist best known for his novel *The Great Gatsby* (1925).

foundryman: a person who works in a foundry, a place where metal goods are made.

Hughes, Langston (1902–67): an American columnist, novelist, playwright, poet, and short story writer. The two volumes of poetry *The Dream Keeper and Other Poems* (1932) and *Montage of a Dream Deferred* (1951) are among his best-known works.

Ku Klux Klan: white supremacist group.

National Association for the Advancement of Colored People (NAACP): a civil rights organization founded in 1909.

pass the bar: fulfill certain requirements in order to be able to practice as a lawyer.

Picasso, Pablo (1881–1973): A Spanish visual artist who pioneered in cubism.

porter: a maintenance worker or baggage handler.

privateer: private person (or that person's ship) commissioned by his or her government during wartime to attack and plunder enemy vessels for a percentage of the loot.

scurvy: a disease caused by a vitamin C deficiency.

Smith, Ada "Bricktop" (1894–1984): an American singer and dancer who had her own nightclub in Paris (1924–61). She was nicknamed "Bricktop" because she was a redhead.

Tuskegee Airmen: the first black pilots in the U.S. armed forces.

Union, the: states and territories that were loyal to the United States during the Civil War.

vaudeville troupe: a group of performers specializing in a type of variety show that typically included singing, dancing, and comic bits.

NOTES

Full citations of works used extensively can be found in Selected Sources.

Preface
page 3 "As you live, believe in Life!": "Du Bois: The Activist Life" scua.library.umass.edu/exhibits/dubois/page14.htm.

Venture Smith, *Prince*
page 5 On Smith's date of birth: Smith's memoir states that he was born about 1729, but scholars now give his date of birth as c. 1727–29.

page 6 On Mumford: Smith's memoir says that his first name was "Robertson," but scholars now know that it was "Robinson."

page 6 "with his own private venture": Venture Smith, *A Narrative . . .* , facsimile in James Brewer Stewart, ed., *Venture Smith and the Business of Slavery and Freedom*, 13.

page 6 "spun money out of sweat": Marilyn Nelson, "Farm Garden," in *The Freedom Business, including A Narrative of the Life & Adventures of Venture, a Native of Africa*, illustrated by Deborah Dancy (Honesdale, Pa.: Boyds Mills Wordsong, 2008): 61.

page 6 Purchasing power of seventy-one pounds and two shillings: Saint and Krimsky, *Making Freedom*, 66.

page 7 "on the ridge . . .": Saint and Krimsky, *Making Freedom*, 84.

page 8 "I left Col. Smith once for all": Venture Smith, *A Narrative . . .* , facsimile in Stewart, ed., *Venture Smith and the Business of Slavery and Freedom*, 24.

page 8 "I was born at Dukandarra . . . globe": Venture Smith, *A Narrative . . .* , facsimile in Stewart, ed. *Venture Smith and the Business of Slavery and Freedom*, 5.

James Forten, *Entrepreneur*
page 12 "I have been taken . . .": Julie Winch, *A Gentleman of Color*, 46.

page 15 "all was order and harmony": W., "A Noble Example," *The Anti-Slavery Record*, December 1835, 150.

page 15 Forten's worth: Lerone Bennett Jr., "The Black Pioneer Period," *Ebony*, November 1970, 66.

page 15 "Death of an Excellent Man": *The North American and Daily Advertiser*, March 5, 1842, 2.

Richard Potter, *Magician*
page 18 "He will present a dollar . . .": "Ventriloquism," *Orange County Patriot*, July 2, 1811, 3.

page 18 a pound of coffee: "The History of What Things Cost in America: 1776 to Today," 24/7 Wall Street, September 16, 2010, 247wallst.com /investing/2010/09/16/the-history-of-what -things-cost-in-america-1776-to-today

page 18 "endless supplies . . . ghostly assistants": Oliver Wendell Holmes, *Over the Teacups* (Boston: Houghton, Mifflin and Co., 1891), 77.

page 18 "us children . . .": H. K. Oliver, "Richard Potter, the Magician and Ventriloquist," *Boston Evening Journal*, August 7, 1874, 1.

page 20 Ketchum on the Potters: "Richard Potter," *The Granite Monthly*, August 1878, 56–60.

page 20 "half-way between fair and black": William Cooper Nell, "Richard Potter," in *Colored Patriots of the American Revolution* (Boston: Robert F. Wallcut, 1855): 92.

James McCune Smith, *Physician*
page 23 Smith's address and the general's reply: "Address to General Lafayette," www.nyhistory.org/web /africanfreeschool/archive/78742-45v .html?collection=0&view=thumbs.

page 24 "at a forge with the bellows . . .": Henry Highland Garnet, quoted in John Stauffer, *The Works of James McCune Smith*, xx.

page 26 "fine breeze . . . beautiful foam-crests": "Dr. Smith's Journal," *Colored American*, November 11, 1837, 3.

page 26 "whirling down the mazy dance": "Dr. Smith's Journal," *Colored American*, March 16, 1839, 2.

page 27 "Medical cures . . . Leeching": ads in *Colored American*, November 18, 1837, 3.

page 27 "foremost . . . and support": Frederick Douglass, *Life and Times of Frederick Douglass* (Hartford, Conn.: Park Publishing Co., 1881), 475.

Mary Bowser, *Spy*

page 29 "one of the highest-placed . . .": Herbert C. Covey and Dwight Eisnach, *How the Slaves Saw the Civil War: Recollections of the War Through the WPA Slave Narratives* (Santa Barbara: ABC-CLIO, 2014), 204.

page 29 "Mary Jane, a colored child. . .": Elizabeth R. Varon, *Southern Lady, Yankee Spy*, 22.

page 31 "You have sent me . . .": William Gilmore Beymer, "Miss Van Lew," *Harper's Monthly*, June 1911, 86.

page 32 "connected with the secret . . . adventures": "Lecture by a Colored Lady," *New York Times*, September 10, 1865, www.nytimes.com/1865/09/10/news /general-city-news.html.

page 32 "on many occasions": "Miss Richmonia Richards's Lecture," *New York Tribune*, September 12, 1865, 4.

page 32 "have repeatedly threaded . . .": "Services of Colored Men," *Douglass' Monthly*, July 1862, 675.

page 32 On Scobell: P. K. Rose, "Black Dispatches: Black American Contributions to Union Intelligence During the Civil War," www.cia.gov/library/center-for-the -study-of-intelligence/csi-publications

/books-and-monographs/black-dispatches, and G. Allen Foster, "John Scobell—Union Spy in Civil War," *Ebony*, October 1978, 73ff.

Allen Allensworth, *Town Founder*

page 36 "crept over to . . . with the comb": Charles Alexander, *Battles and Victories of Allen Allensworth*, 18.

page 36 "a series of persecutions . . .": ibid., 31.

page 36 "I was denuded . . .": ibid., 33.

page 39 "If it had not been for the Negro Cavalry . . .": Edward Austin Johnson, *History of Negro Soldiers in the Spanish-American War: And Other Items of Interest* (Raleigh, N.C.: Capital Printing Company, 1899), 85.

Clara Brown, *Pioneer*

page 43 "a hospital, a hotel, and general refuge . . .": "Aunt Clara Brown," *Kansas City Star*, October 30, 1885, 1.

page 44 "who has been lying . . .": "Death of a Pioneer," *Rocky Mountain News*, October 27, 1885, 6.

page 44 "She could use a four-horse lash . . .": "Cascade Is Joyful on Mary's Birthday," *Anaconda Standard*, April 7, 1913, 4.

Sissieretta Jones, *Concert Singer*

page 48 "I can never remember . . . I loved music": "Is a Singer by Nature," *San Francisco Call*, July 4, 1896, 5.

page 48 Jones's earnings: Maureen D. Lee, *Sissieretta Jones*, Kindle location 1732 of 7566.

page 48 "Her voice is clear and true . . .": from the *Berliner Fremdenblatt*, February 20, 1895, quoted in "Mme. Sisserretta [sic] Jones," (Indianapolis) Freeman, May 4, 1895, 1.

page 50 "The applause . . . own sake alone": John Graziano, "The Early Life and Career of the 'Black Patti,'" 583.

page 50 "Try to hide . . . for an evening": "Is a Singer by Nature," *San Francisco Call*, July 4, 1896, 5.

Maggie Lena Walker, *Bank Founder*

page 53 "Let us put our moneys together . . . into dollars": "The St Luke Penny Savings Bank," www.nps.gov/mawa/the-st-luke-penny-savings-bank.htm.

page 54 "I was not born with a silver spoon . . .": Gertrude Woodruff Marlowe, *A Right Worthy Grand Mission*, 5.

page 55 "As the twig . . .": Marlowe, ibid., 40.

Charlie Wiggins, *Race Car Driver*

page 59 "This auto race will be . . . glory for their Race": Todd Gould, *For Gold and Glory*, 42.

page 60 a dollar's purchasing power: the price of a sirloin steak was 66–75 cents per Table 1 in "Yearly Relative Retail Prices of Food, 1907 to 1916," in *Bulletin of the United States Bureau of Labor Statistics*, No. 228, December 1916, 7.

page 61 "He could just tell by the sound": Gould, *For Gold and Glory*, 10.

page 61 "This is a white man's war": Gould, ibid., 19.

page 63 "He just wouldn't give up . . . with him.": *For Gold and Glory* documentary transcript, www.pbs.org/forgoldandglory/about/transcript.html.

pages 63–64 "Black and white drivers . . .": Gould, *For Gold and Glory*, 165.

page 64 "You couldn't see ten feet in front of you": Gould, ibid., 168.

page 64 "My God! My Charlie. My God!": Gould, ibid., 170.

page 64 "melting into a mountain . . .": Gould, ibid., 169.

page 64 Taylor's "A Dozen Don'ts": www.majortaylorassociation.org/clean_living.shtml.

Eugene Bullard, *Combat Pilot*

page 67 "I wasn't quite sure . . .": Craig Lloyd, *Eugene Bullard*, 37.

page 68 "could never be . . . live in France": Lloyd, *Eugene Bullard*, 36.

page 69 "Chicago slaughter house": Lloyd, *Eugene Bullard*, 44.

Oscar Micheaux, *Filmmaker*

page 76 "I am here to make good . . .": Patrick McGilligan, *Oscar Micheaux*, 38.

page 79 "The super-production, 'The Homesteader' . . .": "Homesteader at Temple Theater Making Hit," *New Orleans Item*, June 26, 1919, 9.

page 79 "one of the most remarkable . . .": "The Homesteader," *Washington Bee*, August 23, 1919, 4.

page 79 "a splendid production": quoted in John Milton Cooper Jr., ed. *Reconsidering Woodrow Wilson: Progressivism, Internationalism, War, and Peace* (Baltimore, Md.: Johns Hopkins University Press, 2008), 121.

page 80 "I have always tried . . .": McGilligan, *Oscar Micheaux*, 207.

page 80 "film methods that were as idiosyncratic . . .": McGilligan, ibid., 142.

Jackie Ormes, *Cartoonist*

page 84 "Yoo-hoo CHES! . . .": Nancy Goldstein, *Jackie Ormes*, 15.

Sadie Tanner Mossell Alexander, *Economist & Attorney*

page 89 "Not one woman . . . regardless of the indignities": Lia B. Epperson, *Knocking Down Doors*, 13.

page 90 "I couldn't get work . . . colored teachers": ibid., 15.

page 91 "I stayed home . . .": ibid., 17.

page 91 On the number of women lawyers: According to Epperson, by 1910 the United States had 558 women lawyers and by 1930 3,385 and only 22 black American women lawyers have been identified from 1872 to

1930 (*Knocking Down Doors*, 5–6).
page 92 "Don't let anything stop you . . .":
Epperson, *Knocking Down Doors*, 1.

Paul R. Williams, *Architect*

pages 95–96 "who ever heard of . . . being
defeated": Paul R. Williams, "I Am a Negro,"
The American Magazine, July 1937, 161.
page 96 "art school 'hopping'": Paul R.
Williams, "If I Were Young Today," *Ebony*,
August 1963, 56.
page 96 "useless ornaments or expensive
fads": "Winners of $5,000 Hollow Tile House
Competition," *The Architect and Engineer*, 60,
no. 1, (January 1920): 68.
page 97 "the great step": "I Am a Negro,"
The American Magazine, July 1937, 161.
page 97 "I could see many . . . a huge
mansion": ibid., 161, 162.
page 98 meetings with E. L. Cord: ibid., 162.

Katherine Coleman Goble Johnson, *Mathematician*

page 103 "I was born liking math . . . I
counted everything": Nancy Feigenbaum,
"Inspiration from the Stars," *Daily Press*,
June 4, 1998, articles.dailypress.com/1998
-06-04/features/9806030288_1_johnsons
-father-space-station-katherine-johnson
page 104 "A wonderful teacher": Wini
Warren, "Katherine Coleman Goble Johnson,"
in *Black Women Scientists in the United States*,
141.
page 104 "You'd make a good . . . You'll find
out": Jim Hodges, "She Was a Computer
When Computers Wore Skirts": www.nasa
.gov/centers/langley/news/researchernews
/rn_kjohnson.html.
page 105 "computers wore skirts": ibid.
page 106 "Everything was so new . . . had to
write them.": Warren, "Katherine Coleman
Goble Johnson," in *Black Women Scientists in
the United States*, 143.

SELECTED SOURCES

Abbott, Karen. *Liar, Temptress, Soldier, Spy: Four Women Undercover in the Civil War.* New York: HarperCollins, 2014.

Alexander, Charles. *Battles and Victories of Allen Allensworth.* Boston: Sherman, French & Company, 1914.

Deiss, Heather S. "Katherine Johnson: A Lifetime of STEM." NASA Educational Technology Services, November 6, 2013. www.nasa.gov/audience /foreducators/a-lifetime-of-stem.html#.

Epperson, Lia B. *Knocking Down Doors: The Trailblazing Life of Sadie Tanner Mossell Alexander, Pennsylvania's First Black Woman Lawyer.* Stanford, Calif.: Women's Legal History Biography Project, Stanford University Law School, 1998. wlh-static.law.stanford.edu/papers /Alexander-epperson98.pdf.

Foster, G. Allen. "John Scobell—Union Spy in Civil War." *Ebony*, October 1978, 73ff.

Goldstein, Nancy. *Jackie Ormes: The First African American Woman Cartoonist.* Ann Arbor: University of Michigan Press, 2008.

Gould, Todd. *For Gold and Glory: Charlie Wiggins and the African-American Racing Car Circuit.* Bloomington: Indiana University Press, 2002.

Graziano, John. "The Early Life and Career of the 'Black Patti': The Odyssey of an African American Singer in the Late Nineteenth Century." *Journal of the American Musicological Society*, vol. 53, no. 3 (2000), 543–96.

Heller, Paul. "The Wizard of Potter Place." *Kearsarge Magazine*, Fall 2010, 35–36.

HistoryMakers, The. "Katherine G. Johnson," Interview February 6, 2012. www .thehistorymakers.com/biography /katherine-g-johnson-42.

Hudson, Karen E. Paul R. Williams, *Architect: A Legacy of Style.* New York: Rizzoli, 1993.

———. Paul R. Williams: *Classic Hollywood Style.* New York: Rizzoli, 2012.

Lee, Maureen D. *Sissieretta Jones: "The Greatest Singer of Her Race," 1868–1933.* Columbia, S.C.: University of South Carolina Press, 2012. Kindle edition.

Leveen, Lois. "Mary Richards Bowser (fl. 1846–1867)." *Encyclopedia Virginia*. Virginia Foundation for the Humanities, 15 Jan 2015. Web. 7 Aug. 2015. www.encyclopediavirginia.org /Bowser_Mary_Richards_fl_1846-1867.

Lloyd, Craig. *Eugene Bullard: Black Expatriate in Jazz-Age Paris.* Athens: University of Georgia Press, 2000.

Makers Team. "Katherine G. Johnson, NASA Mathematician." Audio interview. www .makers.com/katherine-g-johnson.

Marlowe, Gertrude Woodruff. *A Right Worthy Grand Mission: Maggie Lena Walker and the Quest for Black Economic Empowerment.* Washington, D.C.: Howard University Press, 2003.

McGilligan, Patrick. *Oscar Micheaux: The Great and Only: The Life of America's First Black Filmmaker.* New York: HarperCollins, 2007. Kindle edition.

Moody, Joycelyn K., ed. *Memoirs of Elleanor Eldridge.* Morgantown: West Virginia University Press, 2014. Epub.

Morgan, Thomas M., MD. "The Education and Medical Practice of Dr. James McCune Smith (1813–1865), First Black American to Hold a Medical Degree." *Journal of the National Medical Association*, vol. 95, no. 7 (2003), 603–14.

Pecor, Charles J. *The Ten Year Tour of John Rannie: A Magician-Ventriloquist in Early America.* Glenwood, Ill: David Meyer Magic Books, 1998.

SELECTED SOURCES

Peterson, Carla L. *Black Gotham: A Family History of African Americans in Nineteenth-Century New York City*. New Haven, Conn.: Yale University Press, 2011. Kindle edition.

Rose, P. K. "Black Dispatches: Black American Contributions to Union Intelligence During the Civil War." Center for the Study of Intelligence, CIA, posted March 16, 2007, 08:49 AM, last updated: July 7, 2008, 10:18 AM. www.cia.gov /library/center-for-the-study-of -intelligence/csi-publications/books-and -monographs/black-dispatches/index.html.

Royal, Alice C., with Mickey Ellinger and Scott Braley. *Allensworth, The Freedom Colony: A California African American Township*. Berkeley: Heyday Books, 2008.

Saint, Chandler B., and George A. Krimsky. *Making Freedom: The Extraordinary Life of Venture Smith*. Middletown, Conn.: Wesleyan University Press, 2009.

Samuel, Colleen Benham. "Black Magic," *American Legacy*, Spring 2001, 29ff.

Stauffer, John. *The Black Hearts of Men: Radical Abolitionists and the Transformation of Race*. Cambridge, Mass.: Harvard University Press, 2004. Kindle edition.

———, ed. *The Works of James McCune Smith: Black Intellectual and Abolitionist*. New York: Oxford University Press, 2006.

Stewart, James Brewer, ed. *Venture Smith and the Business of Slavery and Freedom*. Amherst: University of Massachusetts Press, 2010.

University of Memphis Art Museum: The Paul Revere Williams Project. www .paulrwilliamsproject.org.

Varon, Elizabeth R. *Southern Lady, Yankee Spy: The True Story of Elizabeth Van Lew, a Union Agent in the Heart of the Confederacy*. New York: Oxford University Press, 2003.

Warren, Wini. *Black Women Scientists in the United States*. Bloomington: Indiana University Press, 1999.

Williams, Paul [R.] "I Am a Negro," *American Magazine*, July 1937, 59, 161–63.

———. "If I Were Young Today," *Ebony*, August 1963, 56.

Winch, Julie. *A Gentleman of Color: The Life of James Forten*. New York: Oxford University Press, 2002. Kindle edition.

IMAGE CREDITS

Case *(front)*: From the University Archives and Records Center, University of Pennsylvania, and Dr. Rae Alexander-Minter. **Case** *(back)*: South Dakota State Historical Society. **Case** *(spine)*: *(from top)* H. Lawrence Freeman Collection, Rare Book and Manuscript Library, Columbia University; Courtesy of California State Parks, 2016, Image 090-2201; DuSable Museum Collection; South Dakota State Historical Society; From the University Archives and Records Center, University of Pennsylvania, and Dr. Rae Alexander-Minter; Courtesy National Park Service, Maggie L. Walker National Historic Site. **Page ii:** Art © Heirs of Aaron Douglas/Licensed by VAGA, New York, NY, and The Fine Arts Museums of San Francisco, museum purchase, the estate of Thurlow E. Tibbs Jr., the Museum Society Auxiliary, American Art Trust Fund, Unrestricted Art Trust Fund, partial gift of Dr. Ernest A. Bates, Sharon Bell, Jo-Ann Beverly, Barbara Carleton, Dr. and Mrs. Arthur H. Coleman, Dr. and Mrs. Coyness Ennix, Jr., Nicole Y. Ennix, Mr. and Mrs. Gary Francois, Dennis L. Franklin, Mr. and Mrs. Maxwell C. Gillette, Mr. and Mrs. Richard Goodyear, Zuretti L. Goosby, Marion E. Greene, Mrs. Vivian S. W. Hambrick, Laurie Gibbs Harris, Arlene Hollis, Louis A. and Letha Jeanpierre, Daniel and Jackie Johnson, Jr., Stephen L. Johnson, Mr. and Mrs. Arthur Lathan, Lewis & Ribbs Mortuary Garden Chapel, Mr. and Mrs. Gary Love, Glenn R. Nance, Mr. and Mrs. Harry S. Parker III, Mr. and Mrs. Carr T. Preston, Fannie Preston, Pamela R. Ransom, Dr. and Mrs. Benjamin F. Reed, San Francisco Black Chamber of Commerce, San Francisco Chapter of Links, Inc., San Francisco Chapter of the N.A.A.C.P., Sigma Pi Phi Fraternity, Dr. Ella Mae Simmons, Mr. Calvin R. Swinson, Joseph B. Williams, Mr. and Mrs. Alfred S. Wilsey, and the people of the Bay Area, 1997.84. **Page 4:** Wesleyan University Library, Special Collections & Archives. **Page 7:** Author's collection *(top)* and Beinecke Rare Book and Manuscript Library, Yale University *(bottom)*. **Page 9:** © David C. Nelson. **Page 10**: Collection of George R. Rinhart. **Page 12:** Author's collection. **Page 14:** Library of Congress. **Page 15:** Author's collection. **Page 16:** Library of Congress. **Page 19:** Library of Congress. **Page 20:** Andover Historical Society. **Page 21:** Historic Northampton, Northampton, Massachusetts. **Page 22:** Photographs and Prints Division, Schomburg Center for Research in Black Culture, The New York Public Library, Astor, Lenox and Tilden Foundations. **Page 24:** Photographs and Prints Division, Schomburg Center for Research in Black Culture, The New York Public Library, Astor, Lenox and Tilden Foundations. **Page 25:** © The Hunterian, University of Glasgow 2015. **Page 27:** Emmet Collection, Miriam and Ira D. Wallach Division of Art, Prints and Photographs, The New York Public Library, Astor, Lenox and Tilden Foundations. **Page 28:** Author's collection. **Page 30:** Library of Congress. **Page 31:** Dickinson College, Archives and Special Collections. **Page 33:** Author's collection. **Page 34:** Courtesy of California State Parks, 2016, Image 090-2201. **Page 36:** Library of Congress. **Page 37:** Author's collection. **Page 39:** Buffalo Bill Center of the West, Cody, Wyoming, U.S.A.; 1.69.5750. **Page 40:** (Scan # 10027902), History Colorado. **Pages 42 and 43:** Library of Congress. **Page 45:** Gilpin Historical Society. **Page 46:** H. Lawrence Freeman Collection, Rare Book and Manuscript Library, Columbia University.

Page 48: Courtesy of the Moorland-Spingarn Research Center, Howard University Archives, Howard University, Washington, D.C. **Page 49:** Library of Congress. **Page 51:** Collection of Marshall Wyatt, Old Hat Records. **Pages 52 and 55:** Courtesy National Park Service, Maggie L. Walker National Historic Site. **Page 57:** Special Collections and Archives, VCU Libraries. **Page 58:** Todd Gould. **Page 60:** Library of Congress. **Page 61:** Racemaker Archive, Fred Roe Collection. **Page 62:** Courtesy Lilly Library, Indiana University, Bloomington, Indiana, and the *Indianapolis Recorder*. **Page 65:** Todd Gould. **Page 66:** National Museum of the U.S. Air Force. **Page 69:** Library of Congress. **Page 70:** National Museum of the U.S. Air Force. **Page 71:** Author's collection. **Page 73:** National Museum of the U.S. Air Force. **Page 74:** South Dakota State Historical Society. **Page 77:** Library of Congress. **Page 78:** From the Edward Mapp Collection of the Margaret Herrick Library, Academy of Motion Picture Arts and Sciences. **Page 80:** General Research & Reference Division, Schomburg Center for Research in Black Culture, The New York Public Library, Astor, Lenox and Tilden Foundations. **Page 81:** Author's collection. **Pages 82 and 84:** DuSable Museum Collection. **Page 85:** *Jackie Ormes: The First African American Woman Cartoonist* by Nancy Goldstein. **Page 86:** Pittsburgh Courier Archives and Sam Milai Collection, The Ohio State University Billy Ireland Cartoon Library & Museum. **Page 87:** Pittsburgh Courier Archives. **Pages 88, 90, 91, and 93:** From the University Archives and Records Center, University of Pennsylvania, and Dr. Rae Alexander-Minter. **Page 94:** Security Pacific National Bank Collection/Los Angeles Public Library. **Page 97:** State Library of New South Wales. **Page 98:** WPA Collection/Los Angeles Public Library. **Page 101:** © J. Paul Getty Trust. Getty Research Institute, Los Angeles (2004.R.10). **Page 102:** Katherine Johnson. **Page 104:** NASA *(top)* and Katherine Johnson *(bottom)*. **Pages 106 and 107:** NASA. **Page 109:** Rosalie O'Connor/American Ballet Theatre.

ACKNOWLEDGMENTS

Thank you, Joylette Hylick, for all your help with my entry on your mother, Katherine Johnson; Todd Gould, for your generosity of spirit and for your grand book *For Gold and Glory: Charlie Wiggins and the African-American Racing Car Circuit*; Nancy Goldstein, for providing information on Ormes images and for your glorious book *Jackie Ormes: The First African American Woman Cartoonist*; David Forsyth, executive director and curator of Gilpin Historical Society, for clarifying some things about Clara Brown; Ethan Bullard, curator of the Maggie Lena Walker National Historic Site, for reviewing my Walker entry and for providing some information I did not know; Nelta (my sister), for the hours spent helping me secure images and clear permissions.

Ever grateful to the marvelous people at Abrams Books for Young Readers: my editor, Howard Reeves; assistant editor, Orlando Dos Reis; copyeditor, Renée Cafiero; proofreader, Zach Greenwald; fact-checker, David M. Webster; managing editor, James Armstrong; associate production director, Alison Gervais; designer, John Clifford; associate art director, Maria T. Middleton; and executive director of publicity and marketing, Jason Wells. It's always so wonderful to work with all of you.

And to my agent, Jennifer Lyons: I thank you so much for all that you do.

INDEX

INDEX

INDEX

INDEX